The Living Trust Book 2026

The Ultimate Estate Planning Guide to Avoid Probate, Protect Your Family, and Set Up a Revocable Living Trust

Thomas R. Irwin

The Living Trust Book 2026
The Ultimate Estate Planning Guide to Avoid Probate, Protect Your Family, and Set Up a Revocable Living Trust

Printed in the United States of America
First Edition: 2026

Contents

Contents (Continued)

INTRODUCTION

Why Living Trusts Matter in 2026

PLANNING FOR THE LONG-TERM SECURITY of your family represents a fundamental step in organizing your personal and financial affairs. Creating an estate plan early in life ensures that your accumulated assets are managed and distributed in complete accordance with your personal values. A primary tool in this coordinate effort is the revocable living trust, which establishes a stable, private framework for asset preservation. This active legal entity holds title to your real estate, bank accounts, and investment portfolios while allowing you to maintain full operational control during your lifetime. By documenting your intentions in a thorough instrument, you prepare a secure foundation that protects your loved ones and supports their future development.

The daily administration of a living trust remains straightforward and integrated with your existing financial routine. You retain the legal capacity to manage your accounts, sell real property, and adjust investment holdings with standard ease. The trust agreement simply designates a successor trustee to step in and assume management authority if you experience a temporary health transition or incapacity. This proactive arrangement provides immediate continuity, ensuring that household expenses are paid and financial transactions proceed without delay. Securing this fiduciary representation guarantees that your affairs are managed by trusted individuals who are legally bound to act solely in your best interest.

This introductory guide is designed to clarify the core concepts of modern estate organization and explain how families can protect their legacy through coordinate planning. Settling an estate through the default legal channels typically requires a public, court-supervised process known as probate which involves public court filings, notice periods, and administrative fees. Establishing a fully funded revocable living trust allows your family to avoid this court-supervised administration entirely, facilitating a private, direct transfer of assets to your beneficiaries. Before finalizing your estate plan, you can utilize the accompanying review checklist to organize your trust, will, powers of attorney, health care documents, beneficiary forms, and asset titles. Ensuring that each of these essential elements is fully coordinated through this systematic checklist protects your family from administrative gaps and guarantees that your legal wishes are executed with complete alignment.

Estate Planning Review Checklist:

- ☐ Revocable Living Trust
- ☐ Last Will and Testament
- ☐ Financial and Durable Powers of Attorney
- ☐ Health Care Proxies and Directives
- ☐ Account Beneficiary Designation Forms
- ☐ Real Estate Deeds and Asset Titles

Ultimately, a well-funded trust provides a harmonious transition that honors your life's work and secures your family's future comfort. Regular reviews of your trust agreement and asset titles ensure that your estate plan remains fully aligned with your current relationships and financial goals. This ongoing attention keeps your planning assets active and protected, giving you and your loved ones complete peace of mind.

PART 1

Estate Planning Foundations

A beginner-friendly introduction to estate planning, probate, wills, trusts, and why planning ahead protects both property and family relationships.

CHAPTER 1

What Estate Planning Really Means

ESTABLISHING A COMPREHENSIVE ESTATE PLAN represents a fundamental step in organizing personal affairs and protecting family members. Every individual possesses assets, ranging from personal belongings and bank accounts to vehicles and residential properties, all of which require clear instructions regarding their future management. This process allows individuals to establish a legal framework that dictates how their property will be distributed, who will make critical medical decisions on their behalf if they become incapacitated, and who will care for minor children. By utilizing formal legal documents, individuals ensure that their preferences are respected and executed in an orderly manner. This structured approach to future planning is accessible to anyone who wishes to provide stability and clarity for their loved ones. Implementing these legal protections is a practical measure for managing everyday assets and personal affairs, ensuring that families are spared from unnecessary administrative confusion during times of transition. Creating these documents provides immediate clarity, allowing families to navigate future events with confidence, certainty, and a clear understanding of their defined roles.

> **Estate planning** is the proactive process of executing legal directives and property arrangements to manage an individual's assets, healthcare choices, and personal wishes during life and after death.

DOCUMENT SPOTLIGHT: THE REVOCABLE LIVING TRUST

Purpose: To hold legal title to assets during your lifetime and facilitate their private, court-free transfer to designated beneficiaries.

Key Authority: This legal vehicle operates immediately upon signing and funding, serving as a private holding entity that remains active and unaffected by the physical status of the grantor.

The Core Elements of Asset Protection

Comprehensive planning relies on a combination of essential legal tools designed to address different scenarios of life and transition. While a living trust manages property distribution privately, other documents focus on personal welfare and physical well-being. A durable power of attorney authorizes a trusted individual to manage financial transactions if the creator of the document is temporarily or permanently unable to do so. Similarly, a healthcare proxy designates a representative to make medical decisions based on the creator's expressed values and treatment preferences. Together, these documents form a protective shield around an individual's life work and personal autonomy. This complete coverage ensures that both financial assets and personal care are managed by individuals who have been deliberately selected and fully prepared for their responsibilities. Engaging in this preparation allows families to remain united and focused on mutual support, secure in the knowledge that all legal contingencies have been thoroughly addressed. Developing these protective measures establishes a reliable foundation, allowing individuals to designate specific responsibilities to trusted advocates.

(!) **Common Mistake:** Assuming estate planning is reserved exclusively for wealthy individuals. Every adult benefits from establishing basic healthcare proxies and financial powers of attorney, regardless of their net worth.

Practical Planning for Everyday Families

Many families begin their planning journey by listing their current assets, such as savings accounts, life insurance policies, and residential property. This inventory helps determine which planning tools will best serve their goals. For families with minor children, naming a guardian is often the most critical decision, ensuring that trusted individuals are legally designated to provide care. This deliberate choice provides parents with immense peace of mind.

STATE LAW REMINDER

> *"State statutes govern the default rules for asset distribution if no formal plan exists. These default rules are standardized and do not account for individual family dynamics or personal relationships."*

Once the primary decisions are made, working with a qualified professional ensures that all documents comply with current state regulations. Regularly reviewing and updating these documents is equally important, particularly after major life events such as marriages, births, or changes in property ownership. Consistent updates maintain the effectiveness of the plan over time, keeping the legal framework fully aligned with the family's evolving needs.

— KEY TAKEAWAY —

Universal Relevance: Every individual has personal wishes and assets that require formal protection, making planning essential for all adults.

Comprehensive Tools: A complete plan includes financial powers of attorney and healthcare directives alongside property distribution documents.

Regular Updates: Reviewing your estate plan every three to five years keeps the documentation accurate and legally binding.

CHAPTER 2

What Happens When You Die Without a Plan

CHOOSING TO POSTPONE the creation of an estate plan leaves the future of family assets and personal decisions entirely in the hands of the state legal system. When an individual passes away without executing a valid Last Will and Testament or a Revocable Living Trust, their estate is classified as intestate. Under the rules of intestacy, the local probate court assumes control over the administration of the estate, appointing an administrator to oversee the process. This court-appointed representative is bound strictly by state statutes, which govern the estate regardless of any informal conversations or unexecuted personal wishes. Consequently, the family must navigate a structured and highly formal legal process to access bank accounts and transfer property titles. This lack of pre-established instruction frequently leads to administrative delays, keeping assets frozen when family members need them most. Establishing a plan ensures that the court system is not required to intervene in private family matters during a time of bereavement. It offers a clear, direct path forward that honors the relationships and commitments built over a lifetime.

Intestacy is the legal state of passing away without a valid will or trust, which triggers the automatic application of state laws to distribute the deceased's assets.

DOCUMENT SPOTLIGHT: LETTERS OF ADMINISTRATION

Purpose: A formal court document issued to an administrator authorizing them to manage and distribute an intestate estate.

Key Authority: This document gives the court-appointed representative the legal power to access financial accounts, sell real property, and pay outstanding debts under direct judicial supervision.

The Burden of Intestate Succession

Standard state formulas distribute assets among biological relatives, which may exclude close friends, dedicated caregivers, or favorite charitable organizations. Furthermore, the state distribution plan may divide assets in ways that create logistical hardships for the surviving family. Joint ownership of a family home might be split between a surviving spouse and children from a previous marriage, leading to potential disagreements regarding the property's management or sale. This process demonstrates the value of proactive planning to ensure that personal intentions govern asset distribution, protecting surviving relatives from administrative stress and unnecessary legal disputes. Relying on informal promises or general expectations often complicates this process, highlighting the importance of formal legal arrangements.

Common Mistake: Assuming that assets will automatically transfer to a surviving spouse without court involvement. Most states divide intestate property between the spouse and children, requiring formal probate oversight.

Family Harmony and Structural Clarity

In addition to financial assets, intestate proceedings can create significant uncertainty regarding the custody of minor children. If both parents pass away without naming a legal guardian, the probate court must select a guardian based on state guidelines and testimony from relatives. This judicial selection process can lead to emotional disagreements among well-meaning family members, as multiple parties may believe they are best suited to raise the children.

STATE LAW REMINDER

"Intestacy rules are governed exclusively by the laws of the state where you reside at the time of death, or where real property is physically located, leading to inconsistent distribution rules across borders."

The administrative burden placed on grieving family members during an intestate probate process is substantial. Family members must locate assets, identify legal heirs, notify creditors, and attend court hearings, all while managing their personal grief. Providing a clear estate plan removes this weight from their shoulders, offering a structured path that preserves family harmony and ensures a peaceful, organized transition of responsibilities.

— KEY TAKEAWAY —

Statutory Distribution: Dying without a plan permits state statutes to determine who inherits your property and cares for minor children.

Increased Expenses: Intestate estates often incur higher court fees and administrative costs, which directly reduce the legacy left for family members.

Delayed Distribution: Resolving an intestate estate through the court system takes months, or even years, delaying the financial support your loved ones may need.

CHAPTER 3

Probate Explained in Plain English

PROBATE IS THE FORMAL, court-supervised legal process designed to validate an individual's Last Will and Testament, identify and appraise their assets, pay outstanding debts, and distribute the remaining property to beneficiaries. Historically, this system was established to protect creditors and ensure that an estate's transition occurred in an orderly, legal manner under public scrutiny. When a person passes away, the nominated executor must petition the local probate court to open the estate and receive official permission to act. This process requires submitting the original will, filing inventory reports of all assets, and publishing public notices to allow creditors to make claims. Because the court must verify every step, the entire administration is subject to procedural delays and strict timelines. The procedural hurdles of probate can feel overwhelming to grieving family members who must manage complex paperwork alongside their loss. Understanding how the probate system functions is the first step toward implementing strategies that simplify the transition and shield family assets from unnecessary court delays. Proactive preparation allows families to manage these requirements efficiently and maintain control over their financial legacy.

> **Probate** is the judicial process whereby a court validates a deceased person's will, supervises the settlement of their debts, and oversees the legal distribution of their remaining assets.

DOCUMENT SPOTLIGHT: THE PETITION FOR PROBATE

Purpose: The initial legal document filed with the court to formally request the opening of probate and the appointment of an executor.

Key Authority: Filing this petition initiates the public legal proceedings, requiring formal notice to all heirs, beneficiaries, and potential creditors according to state law.

The Real-World Impact of Court Supervision

Court-supervised estate settlement introduces several significant drawbacks that lead many families to seek alternative solutions. The most prominent challenges of probate are the associated costs, the time required to complete the process, and the complete loss of privacy. Court filing fees, executor commissions, publication costs, and attorney fees can consume a substantial percentage of the estate's total value, leaving less for the beneficiaries. Additionally, probate is a slow process, often requiring nine months to over a year to fully resolve, during which time assets may be frozen and inaccessible. Because probate is a matter of public record, anyone can access the court files to view the estate's inventory, outstanding debts, and the identities of the beneficiaries. Understanding these challenges empowers families to take control of their financial legacy and implement planning strategies that prioritize privacy and efficiency. Analyzing the statutory requirements of the local court system helps clarify the administrative steps heirs must undertake.

Common Mistake: Believing that having a Will allows your family to avoid probate. In fact, a Will must go through the probate court to be validated and executed.

Creating a Path Around the Courtroom

Fortunately, modern estate planning offers several reliable methods to transfer assets directly to loved ones without entering the probate courtroom. Utilizing revocable living trusts, designating transfer-on-death beneficiaries on bank accounts, and establishing joint tenancy with rights of survivorship are effective strategies for bypassing probate. These methods allow ownership of assets to transfer automatically and privately immediately upon death, ensuring that family members have prompt access to financial support.

STATE LAW REMINDER

"Many states offer simplified probate procedures, often called small estate administration, for estates whose total value falls below a specific statutory threshold, reducing the time and cost involved."

Completing a trust plan requires updating each bank account, investment portfolio, and real estate deed to reflect the new ownership or beneficiary designations. This process of alignment ensures that your assets are protected and flow directly to your loved ones according to your precise timeline and instructions.

— KEY TAKEAWAY —

Public Record: Probate is an entirely public process, meaning your family's assets, debts, and distribution plans are accessible to anyone.

Time and Cost: The typical probate process takes nine to twelve months and incurs substantial court and legal fees that diminish the estate's value.

Proactive Alternatives: Utilizing trusts, joint tenancy, and beneficiary designations allows assets to transfer privately and instantly, bypassing court intervention entirely.

CHAPTER 4

The Difference Between a Will and a Trust

ESTABLISHING A RELIABLE LEGAL FRAMEWORK for the eventual transition of family property requires a clear understanding of the distinct functions served by wills and trusts. Every estate consists of personal assets that must eventually be transferred to heirs, and selecting the correct legal instrument is essential to ensure this transfer occurs efficiently. A Last Will and Testament provides a written set of instructions that directs the distribution of individually owned property upon the death of the creator. A revocable living trust represents a separate fiduciary arrangement that holds legal title to assets during the creator's lifetime and permits the private transfer of those assets to beneficiaries. This continuous legal structure remains active during life, during periods of potential medical incapacity, and after death, providing a unified platform for managing personal property. Utilizing these distinct instruments in a coordinated manner establishes a reliable foundation, allowing families to secure their legacy and prepare for future transitions with complete legal clarity.

> A Last Will and Testament is a court-administered directive for distributing personal assets after death. A revocable living trust is an active fiduciary entity that holds title to assets to facilitate their private management and transfer.

DOCUMENT SPOTLIGHT: THE POUR-OVER WILL

Purpose: To serve as a safety device that automatically captures any assets held in an individual's name at death and transfers them into an existing revocable living trust structure.

Key Authority: This specialized will directs the probate court to distribute any individually held property to the trustee of the trust, ensuring a unified asset distribution process.

Judicial Oversight and Private Administration

The administration of a Last Will and Testament requires a formal court process known as probate, during which a judge validates the document and supervises the estate's settlement. This judicial process involves public filings, notice requirements for creditors, and mandatory waiting periods to allow claims to be filed and resolved. The court-appointed executor must present detailed inventory records, pay court fees, and obtain judicial approval before distributing any remaining assets to the beneficiaries listed in the will. The administration of a revocable living trust is managed privately by a successor trustee without the involvement of the court system. Implementing a trust structure provides immediate continuity, protecting family assets from public disclosure and administrative delays during a sensitive period of transition. Failing to understand these operational differences can lead to unexpected administrative hurdles and public exposure of family affairs during estate settlement. Taking the time to evaluate how each tool functions ensures that the transition of assets proceeds exactly as intended without unnecessary stress.

Common Mistake: Assuming that executing a Last Will and Testament avoids the probate court system, when in fact a will must be formally admitted to probate to have legal effect.

The Scope of Asset Control

The effective operation of both wills and trusts depends entirely on the legal title of the assets at the time of the creator's death. A revocable living trust only controls assets that have been formally transferred into the name of the trust, a process known as trust funding.

STATE LAW REMINDER

"Real estate deeds and financial accounts must be formally retitled in the name of the trust to ensure they remain under the authority of the successor trustee and bypass court-supervised administration."

Properly aligning asset titles with the trust agreement requires contacting financial institutions, updating deeds with local county offices, and submitting updated beneficiary forms. This systematic organization simplifies the eventual transition, allowing the successor trustee to manage family property efficiently and in accordance with your precise instructions.

— KEY TAKEAWAY —

Court Process: Wills require formal validation through local probate courts prior to asset distribution.

Immediate Operation: Trusts manage property immediately upon creation and continue seamlessly after the grantor's passing.

Coordinate Funding: Retitling assets remains the essential step to ensure a trust controls and protects family property.

CHAPTER 5

The Main Documents in a Complete Estate Plan

DESIGNING A RESILIENT ESTATE PLAN requires assembling a cohesive portfolio of legal instruments that protect your interests across different areas of life. A complete estate plan addresses property distribution, financial management, medical decision-making, and the personal care of family members during periods of health and incapacity. A Last Will and Testament designates guardians for minor children and distributes individually held property, while a revocable living trust facilitates the private transfer of primary family assets. Financial powers of attorney authorize trusted agents to manage daily transactions, and medical directives establish clear pathways for healthcare decisions if you are unable to communicate. Together, these individual instruments function as an integrated network, providing structural support and practical guidance for your family under any circumstances. Preparing this complete suite of documents establishes a reliable foundation, allowing you to secure your legacy and maintain control over your personal affairs.

> A complete estate plan is an integrated collection of legal instruments that organize property distribution, financial management, and medical decision-making to protect an individual's welfare and legacy during life and after death.

DOCUMENT SPOTLIGHT: DURABLE FINANCIAL POWER OF ATTORNEY

Purpose: To authorize a designated representative to manage banking transactions, sign tax returns, and conduct business affairs on your behalf during periods of physical or medical incapacity.

Key Authority: This document remains legally valid and active if the creator experiences temporary or permanent medical incapacity, preventing court-appointed guardianship.

Healthcare Directives and Personal Autonomy

Financial documents protect property and business interests, and medical directives secure personal well-being and bodily autonomy during medical emergencies. A complete healthcare plan includes a medical power of attorney, also known as a healthcare proxy, which designates a trusted representative to make medical decisions on your behalf. This document is accompanied by a living will, which provides specific instructions regarding medical treatments, life-support preferences, and end-of-life care based on your personal values. These combined directives guide physicians and family members during critical moments, removing the burden of making difficult medical choices without prior guidance. Having these explicit instructions in place ensures that your medical treatment remains aligned with your personal preferences and ethical beliefs. This clear line of decision-making authority protects your physical autonomy, providing family members with absolute clarity when communicating with medical staff during sensitive clinical situations.

(!) **Common Mistake:** Neglecting to coordinate beneficiary designation forms with your primary estate documents, as asset designations on retirement accounts and insurance policies override instructions in a will or trust.

Directives for Daily Administration

A complete estate plan also incorporates practical, non-technical instructions designed to assist your representatives in managing daily administrative tasks. A formal letter of instruction provides a practical guide, detailing the location of vital documents, digital account access information, outstanding liabilities, and specific preferences for personal belongings. It compiles administrative details in a single, accessible document, preventing heirs from searching through files during a stressful transition.

STATE LAW REMINDER

"Medical directives and financial powers of attorney require specific state-approved formats, signature witnesses, and formal notarization to be recognized as valid by local hospitals and financial institutions."

Working with an experienced professional ensures that each administrative document complies with current state statutes and operates successfully within local institutions. Regularly updating these forms is important, especially after changes in health, relationship status, or property ownership. Consolidating these medical, financial, and practical directives alongside your trust and will creates a secure, resilient framework for your family.

— KEY TAKEAWAY —

Decisional Authority: Powers of attorney protect personal and financial decisions during life, while wills and trusts manage property distribution.

Beneficiary Forms: Accounts with designated beneficiaries transfer automatically at death, bypassing instructions in other estate documents.

Practical Guidance: Letters of instruction provide immediate, actionable details regarding digital accounts, locations of assets, and personal wishes.

CHAPTER 6

Common Myths About Living Trusts

IMPLEMENTING A SUCCESSFUL ESTATE PLAN requires clarifying common misunderstandings regarding the legal structure and practical benefits of revocable living trusts. Many individuals believe that establishing a trust is a highly complex process intended only for families with exceptional wealth or unique property holdings. Others assume that a revocable trust automatically provides absolute protection from personal creditors and eliminates all personal tax liabilities during the creator's lifetime. Understanding the true legal status of these documents is essential to design an effective estate plan that meets your family's goals. A revocable living trust is a practical tool designed primarily to avoid the delays of probate court and ensure management continuity during incapacity. Clarifying these legal realities allows families to utilize trusts successfully, protecting their home and primary assets while remaining in full compliance with state and federal guidelines. Establishing this solid foundation replaces standardized defaults with your personalized wishes, ensuring your family has a reliable, structured path forward.

> **A revocable living trust** is a private estate planning instrument designed to bypass the probate court system, maintaining tax neutrality and personal creditor exposure during the grantor's lifetime.

DOCUMENT SPOTLIGHT: THE TRUST FUNDING DEED

Purpose: To formally transfer ownership of real estate from an individual's personal name to the name of their revocable living trust.

Key Authority: This recorded conveyance removes the property from the individual's probate estate, ensuring the home transfers privately and directly to the beneficiaries upon the owner's passing.

Taxation and Creditor Reality

A revocable living trust is a tax-neutral instrument during the creator's lifetime, meaning it does not alter your personal income tax obligations. Because the grantor retains complete control over the trust assets, including the power to amend or revoke the trust at any time, the IRS treats the trust as a grantor trust for income tax reporting. All income, capital gains, and deductions generated by trust assets are reported directly on your personal income tax return using your personal social security number. The trust does not require a separate federal tax identification number or a separate annual tax filing during your lifetime. Similarly, assets held within a revocable trust remain subject to claims from personal creditors, as the law treats the grantor as the actual owner of the property. This structure maintains complete simplicity for annual tax preparation and financial transactions while establishing a reliable, private transfer mechanism for the future. Dispelling these misconceptions is critical for developing a realistic and legally compliant plan that achieves your personal goals. Clear knowledge of trust operations protects families from choosing ineffective shortcuts that do not deliver real protection.

Common Mistake: Believing that a revocable living trust provides an immediate shield against personal lawsuit liability or eliminates personal income tax obligations during the creator's lifetime.

The Limits of Standardized Do-It-Yourself Software

Many families consider using standardized do-it-yourself online templates to draft their trust documents, assuming these forms provide complete legal protection. A poorly structured or improperly executed trust document can create administrative confusion, potentially requiring court intervention to resolve ambiguities after the creator's passing.

STATE LAW REMINDER

"Trust validation and execution standards are governed by state-specific statutes, requiring exact signature, witness, and notary protocols to be legally recognized within your local jurisdiction.
"

Professional legal guidance helps avoid the structural errors often found in generic templates, ensuring that your trust operates seamlessly when needed. This customized preparation guarantees that your home, accounts, and personal legacy are fully secured according to your precise wishes. Regularly updating your trust to reflect changes in property ownership or state law maintains its strength over time.

— KEY TAKEAWAY —

Tax Transparency: Revocable trusts use the grantor's social security number, keeping tax filing straightforward and identical to individual reporting.

Fiduciary Continuity: Trusts provide seamless management of assets if the grantor experiences a medical emergency or physical incapacity.

Thorough Funding: Successful trust administration depends entirely on retitling assets from personal ownership to the name of the trust.

CHAPTER 7

Who Needs an Estate Plan?

PREPARING FOR THE FUTURE is a universal responsibility that offers valuable protection for individuals across all stages of life and financial situations. A common misunderstanding suggests that estate plans are only necessary during retirement or in the presence of substantial wealth. In reality, any adult who owns real estate, cares for minor children, or values personal decision-making benefits from establishing formal legal directives. Homeowners require plans to secure their properties, while parents of minor children must designate legal guardians to ensure continuous care. Retirees, unmarried couples, blended families, and business owners each face specific scenarios that require tailored legal documentation. Creating these custom directives ensures that your personal property is preserved and your loved ones are protected from administrative complications during times of transition. Implementing these legal protections is a practical measure for managing everyday assets and personal affairs, ensuring that families are spared from unnecessary administrative confusion.

> Tailored estate planning is a protective legal framework designed to organize property distribution, name caregivers, and secure decision-making authority for any adult, regardless of estate size.

DOCUMENT SPOTLIGHT: BUSINESS BUY-SELL AGREEMENT

Purpose: To govern the future transfer of co-owned business interests upon the retirement, disability, or passing of a partner.

Key Authority: This binding agreement establishes a pre-arranged buyout structure, protecting business operations and providing financial security for the owner's family.

Protecting Minor Children and Real Estate

For parents of minor children, the formal nomination of a legal guardian is the single most critical decision in the estate planning process. Without a written directive designating a guardian, the local probate court must select a guardian based on standardized state statutes and testimony from relatives. This judicial selection process can lead to emotional family disputes and custody challenges, causing unnecessary stress for the children. Similarly, homeowners require proactive planning to ensure their primary residence transfers directly to their intended heirs. Real estate left in an individual's name must go through the public probate court system, potentially forcing heirs to sell the home to cover court costs and administrative fees. Formally declaring a guardian and utilizing transfer-on-death deeds or living trusts ensures that your children are cared for by trusted individuals and your home is preserved privately for their future. Taking proactive steps early in life establishes a vital safety net that safeguards your family during unpredictable life events. Securing these core protections provides immediate comfort, allowing you and your loved ones to focus on building a bright future together.

!

Common Mistake: Delaying the creation of basic estate planning documents under the assumption that these arrangements are only necessary for senior citizens or wealthy families.

Navigating Complex Family Structures

Specialized planning is particularly important for blended families, unmarried partners, and business owners who face specific challenges under standard state laws. State intestacy laws do not recognize unmarried partners for default asset distribution, meaning that a formal will or trust is required to secure any property transfers between partners. For blended families, structured trusts ensure that a surviving spouse is supported while protecting the long-term inheritance of children from previous relationships. Business owners must also integrate operational succession plans to prevent company liquidation and facilitate a smooth transfer of ownership.

STATE LAW REMINDER

"Unmarried partners must execute explicit wills or trusts to receive assets or make medical decisions, as state laws do not provide default protections for unmarried couples."

Aligning your estate plan with your unique family and business requirements provides a secure, enduring legacy for everyone you care about. Regularly updating these documents ensures they reflect changes in property ownership, family structure, and state regulations, maintaining the effectiveness of your plan over time. Working with an experienced professional allows you to build a secure, legally binding plan that protects your family, home, and business.

— KEY TAKEAWAY —

Guardian Nominations: Parents must explicitly designate legal guardians in writing to secure the future care of minor children.

Partner Protection: Unmarried couples require formal wills or trusts to establish property rights and medical decision-making authority.

Business Succession: Business owners must integrate operational plans to prevent company liquidation and facilitate a smooth transfer of ownership.

PART 2

Understanding Revocable Living Trusts

Explains what a revocable living trust is, how it works, and why it is one of the most common estate planning tools.

CHAPTER 8

What Is a Revocable Living Trust?

ENTERING INTO A FIDUCIARY AGREEMENT provides a secure and reliable platform for organizing family property. This process involves the creation of a written trust agreement that outlines the rules for asset management and eventual distribution. This legal arrangement serves to document your intentions in a thorough manner so that every detail remains perfectly preserved over time. By defining the administrative parameters in a clear instrument, you provide direct guidance for those who will handle your affairs in future years. Each designated individual receives a specific mandate to protect the integrity of the family estate according to the terms you outline. As a result of this meticulous planning, the structural alignment of the trust supports a seamless transition that benefits everyone involved. A revocable living trust is a formal legal structure that holds title to personal assets to protect their transition across generations. Establishing this entity creates a distinct legal framework where ownership is divided into legal and beneficial interests, allowing families to build a secure legacy. Utilizing this structure establishes a reliable foundation, allowing families to prepare for future transitions with complete legal clarity.

> A revocable living trust is a legal entity created by a written agreement to hold and manage assets, defined by the distinct roles of the grantor, trustee, successor trustee, and beneficiary.

DOCUMENT SPOTLIGHT: THE TRUST AGREEMENT

Purpose: To serve as the primary governing document that outlines the rules, distribution instructions, and administrative powers for managing trust assets.

Key Authority: This agreement provides the trustee with the legal capacity to manage, invest, and transfer the property held within the trust's portfolio.

The Core Roles in a Fiduciary Agreement

The creation of a revocable living trust begins with the grantor, who is the individual establishing the entity and transferring assets into it. The grantor determines the terms of the trust, identifying which assets are included and designating how those assets will be managed and distributed. Along with the grantor, the trustee is appointed to hold legal title to the trust property and manage it according to the specific instructions outlined in the trust agreement. In many cases, the grantor serves as the initial trustee during their lifetime, maintaining direct day-to-day administration over the funded assets.

This arrangement ensures that the management of personal property remains simple and directly aligned with the creator's intent. The administrative responsibilities of the trustee require a high standard of care, known as a fiduciary duty, which obligates the trustee to act solely in the best interests of the trust's designated participants. By establishing these clearly defined boundaries, the grantor creates a reliable structure that survives changes in circumstances and supports long-term property administration.

Understanding the legal separation of these roles helps families establish a secure framework for their assets. Clear communication regarding these administrative positions prepares everyone involved for their future responsibilities.

!

Common Mistake: Assuming that the grantor, trustee, and beneficiary must always be separate individuals, when in fact one person can hold all three roles simultaneously during their lifetime.

The Successor Trustee and Beneficiary Relationship

The successor trustee is a crucial role designed to ensure continuity when the original trustee can no longer manage the trust. The successor trustee assumes active administrative control over the trust assets only upon the death, resignation, or incapacity of the initial trustee. This transition occurs privately, allowing the successor trustee to manage bills, invest funds, and distribute property without needing permission from a probate court judge. Beneficiaries hold equitable title to the trust property, possessing the right to enjoy and receive the assets according to the grantor's written instructions.

STATE LAW REMINDER

"State statutes govern the specific duties of a successor trustee, including mandatory accounting requirements and notice provisions that must be sent to all qualified beneficiaries during trust administration."

Properly defining these roles in the trust agreement ensures that your successor trustee understands their legal obligations. Engaging in detailed discussions with your designated successor trustee helps prevent administrative errors and establishes a cooperative relationship with the beneficiaries. This thorough preparation secures your assets and maintains family harmony during future transitions.

— KEY TAKEAWAY —

The Grantor: Specifies the terms of the trust agreement and transfers initial legal title of property into the entity.

Fiduciary Roles: Successor trustees assume control privately to manage and distribute property for the beneficiaries.

Distribution Structure: Beneficiaries receive assets according to the precise terms and timelines set by the grantor.

CHAPTER 9

How a Living Trust Works During Your Lifetime

MAINTAINING COMPLETE PERSONAL CONTROL over your property remains a primary objective of estate planning. A revocable living trust is designed to operate seamlessly during the lifetime of the grantor, ensuring no disruption to your daily affairs. This continuous oversight means that your financial routine proceeds without any additional administrative burdens or procedural changes. You retain the legal capacity to manage bank accounts, execute real estate transactions, and adjust investment portfolios with standard ease. The everyday coordination of your assets remains entirely within your personal preview, providing uninterrupted access to your holdings. This reliable operational layout ensures that the transition to a trust structure supports your ongoing lifestyle and long-term security goals. This legal entity allows the creator to retain total administrative authority over all funded assets while they are alive and mentally capable. The grantor acts as the primary trustee, maintaining the ability to buy, sell, spend, or transfer property exactly as they did before establishing the trust structure.

> Lifetime trust operation is the period during which the grantor retains complete control to manage, amend, or revoke the trust, keeping asset administration simple and personal.

DOCUMENT SPOTLIGHT: THE REVOCATION AMENDMENT

Purpose: To allow the grantor to formally modify, update, or completely dissolve the trust agreement during their lifetime to reflect changing circumstances.

Key Authority: This amendment process permits the creator to add or remove assets, change beneficiaries, or designate new successor trustees at any time.

The Mechanism of Complete Lifelong Control

The defining characteristic of a revocable living trust is its complete flexibility during the grantor's lifetime. Because the trust is revocable, the grantor retains the legal right to alter any terms of the agreement or terminate the trust entirely. For income tax purposes, the internal revenue service considers the trust transparent, allowing all income and capital gains to be reported directly on the grantor's individual tax return. This tax neutrality simplifies ongoing administration, ensuring that establishing a trust does not add complex tax reporting requirements to your daily life.

As the trustee of your own trust, you manage your financial accounts, real estate, and investments with standard administrative ease. Financial institutions recognize the trustee's authority to conduct normal transactions, including opening accounts, purchasing property, and managing investments. This integrated structure ensures that your assets remain fully accessible to you, supporting your lifestyle and financial goals throughout your lifetime.

A clear understanding of this ongoing control provides peace of mind to grantors who want to protect their estate. Recognizing that your daily financial routine remains unchanged helps you approach the funding process with confidence.

!

Common Mistake: Believing that transferring assets into a revocable living trust restricts your personal use of those assets or requires a separate tax identification number during your lifetime.

Managing Assets During Periods of Incapacity

The secondary purpose of a revocable living trust is to provide a clear, pre-arranged path for asset management during periods of medical or physical incapacity. If the grantor experiences a medical emergency that prevents them from managing their financial affairs, the trust agreement outlines a private mechanism for transitioning authority. Under this mechanism, the successor trustee assumes active management of the trust assets without requiring a court-supervised guardianship or conservatorship hearing. The determination of incapacity is guided by specific standards set forth in the agreement, such as written evaluations from licensed physicians, which prevents family disagreements and ensures that the successor trustee can act quickly.

STATE LAW REMINDER

"State laws provide legal protections for incapacitated grantors, ensuring that successor trustees manage trust assets solely for the benefit and medical care of the original grantor during their disability."

Establishing these incapacity provisions in your trust agreement provides a secure layer of protection for your personal welfare. Taking the time to discuss these medical trigger events with your successor trustee ensures they are prepared to step in smoothly. This proactive planning secures your financial independence and provides your family with clear directions under any circumstances.

— KEY TAKEAWAY —

Ongoing Flexibility: Grantors can modify, fund, or revoke the trust agreement at point during their lifetime.

Tax Simplicity: Trust assets are reported under the grantor's social security number, maintaining standard annual tax filing.

Incapacity Protection: Successor trustees step in privately to manage assets during medical emergencies, bypassing court intervention.

CHAPTER 10

How a Living Trust Works After Death

UPON THE PASSING OF THE TRUST CREATOR, the successor trustee assumes immediate administrative authority over the trust assets without judicial oversight. This private administration begins with a thorough inventory of all trust assets to establish their value at the date of death. Setting these values ensures that beneficiaries receive accurate reporting and assists in calculating any potential tax obligations. The successor trustee documents every administrative action in a systematic ledger to maintain complete transparency. Each step of this process is designed to protect the assets from loss or mismanagement during the settlement period. This methodical approach ensures that the trust assets are secure and prepared for distribution. A successor trustee has the legal responsibility to follow the instructions in the trust agreement exactly as written. This transition represents a direct and structured continuation of the grantor's original intentions.

> Post-death trust administration is the private process of settling trust affairs, paying final expenses, and distributing remaining assets to beneficiaries according to the trust agreement.

DOCUMENT SPOTLIGHT: DEATH CERTIFICATE

Purpose: To provide formal verification of the grantor's passing and confirm the successor trustee's active authority to financial institutions.

Key Authority: This combined documentation allows the successor trustee to access trust accounts, retitle real estate properties, and execute final transfers.

THE PRACTICAL PATH OF SUCCESSOR ADMINISTRATION

Settling a trust requires the successor trustee to take several sequential, administrative actions to organize the estate. The successor trustee secures multiple certified copies of the death certificate to submit to financial institutions holding trust accounts. Following this step, the trustee obtains a new federal tax identification number for the trust, as the grantor's social security number is no longer valid for tax reporting. The trustee opens an administrative bank account under this new number to consolidate cash holdings and pay outstanding administrative expenses.

Maintaining meticulous records of all income, expenditures, and asset valuations represents an essential duty of the successor trustee during this transition period. The trustee gathers professional appraisals for real estate holdings and secure market valuations for investment portfolios as of the date of death. This documentation establishes the stepped-up tax basis for the assets, which protects the beneficiaries from unnecessary future tax burdens.

Understanding these detailed administrative steps simplifies the entire settlement process for family members. Providing clear documentation at every stage of administration reduces confusion and helps the successor trustee complete their duties efficiently.

Common Mistake: Delaying the formal appraisal of trust-held real estate at the date of death, which makes calculating the stepped-up basis difficult and complicates tax reporting.

Distributing Assets to Designated Beneficiaries

The final responsibility of the successor trustee involves distributing the remaining trust property to the designated beneficiaries in a timely manner. The trustee reviews the trust agreement to determine if distributions are outright transfers or structured payments held in ongoing sub-trusts. Structured distributions require the trustee to manage the assets continuously, making payments to beneficiaries according to specified ages, milestones, or health requirements.

The distribution process requires a careful review of each beneficiary's circumstances and needs. Providing detailed final reports to all qualified beneficiaries ensures complete clarity and maintains trust within the family. This transparent administration protects the successor trustee from potential liability and completes the settlement process.

STATE LAW REMINDER

"Successor trustees must satisfy all valid estate debts, funeral costs, administrative expenses, and tax liabilities before making final distributions to trust beneficiaries."

Preparing a final accounting and securing written liability releases from beneficiaries represents a prudent step before distributing assets. This systematic documentation confirms that all parties are satisfied with the administration of the estate. Professional guidance throughout this process guarantees full compliance with local regulations and protects the family legacy.

— KEY TAKEAWAY —

Immediate Continuity: Successor trustees take control privately without waiting for probate court approval.

Asset Valuation: Obtaining date-of-death appraisals establishes the stepped-up tax basis for beneficiaries.

Orderly Distribution: Trustees satisfy all valid administrative costs and taxes before transferring assets to heirs.

CHAPTER 11

Revocable vs. Irrevocable Trusts

SELECTING THE APPROPRIATE TRUST VEHICLE requires an analysis of distinct legal structures. Each trust type offers a unique method for managing property during your lifetime and after your passing. Revocable trusts are designed primarily to maintain complete personal control and facilitate a private transfer of assets. Irrevocable trusts are created as independent legal entities to secure specific tax benefits or asset protection. Understanding the operational rules of each structure helps you select the correct instrument for your family's needs. This proactive choice establishes a secure foundation that protects your assets according to your precise plans. The choice between these structures determines the level of control you retain over your transferred property. This decision shapes your overall estate plan, helping you protect your family with complete legal clarity.

> Revocable trusts offer lifetime flexibility and ongoing personal control, while irrevocable trusts require a permanent transfer of assets to achieve separate tax status or creditor insulation.

DOCUMENT SPOTLIGHT: IRREVOCABLE TRUST

Purpose: To establish a permanent estate planning structure that cannot be modified or terminated by the grantor after execution.

Key Authority: This agreement removes the assets permanently from the grantor's personal estate, transferring complete administrative control to an independent trustee.

The Operational Rules of Revocable Structures

A revocable living trust operates under the principle of lifetime flexibility, allowing the grantor to remain in control of all funded assets. The grantor maintains the legal right to amend, update, or completely dissolve the trust agreement at any time. Because of this ongoing access, the assets are considered part of the grantor's personal estate for tax and creditor purposes. Income generated by trust assets is reported directly on the grantor's individual income tax return, keeping annual tax preparation straightforward.

This continuous control ensures that establishing a revocable trust does not disrupt your daily financial activities or banking relationships. You continue to buy, sell, and manage property inside the trust exactly as you did under individual ownership. The primary advantage of this structure remains its ability to bypass the probate court system privately while preserving your absolute freedom of action during your lifetime.

Recognizing the flexible nature of revocable trusts helps families integrate them successfully into their financial plans. This clear understanding ensures that you maintain complete operational comfort while preparing a private transition for your heirs.

Common Mistake: Assuming that a revocable living trust protects assets from personal creditors during your lifetime, when in fact your ongoing control keeps these assets exposed to legal claims.

The permanent Character of Irrevocable trusts

An irrevocable trust operates as a separate legal entity, requiring the grantor to yield control over the transferred property. An independent trustee is appointed to manage the trust property, making investment decisions and distributions according to the terms of the agreement. This complete separation removes the assets from the grantor's personal estate, reducing overall estate tax exposure and providing strong insulation from personal creditor claims. Establishing an irrevocable trust requires a complete transfer of assets and independent administrative oversight. Working with an experienced professional ensures that the trust complies with all federal fiduciary tax guidelines.

STATE LAW REMINDER

"Irrevocable trusts must secure a separate federal employer identification number and file an independent fiduciary income tax return annually to report trust income."

Choosing the correct trust structure requires a thorough review of your family's financial goals, tax profile, and protection needs. Revocable trusts are ideal for families seeking probate avoidance and ongoing control, while irrevocable trusts serve those needing specialized tax planning. Regular consultations with estate planning professionals ensure your choices remain fully aligned with changing regulations.

— KEY TAKEAWAY —

Lifetime Control: Revocable trusts permit continuous modifications, spending, and total access during the grantor's life.

Permanent Separation: Irrevocable trusts transfer property permanently, removing assets from the grantor's taxable estate.

Asset Protection: Irrevocable structures provide creditor protection by separating the grantor from ownership and control.

CHAPTER 12

What a Living Trust Can and Cannot Do

ACHIEVING REALISTIC PLANNING OBJECTIVES requires a clear understanding of your chosen legal instruments. A basic revocable living trust performs specific administrative functions with exceptional efficiency and reliability. This structure is designed to hold your primary assets, simplify lifetime management, and bypass the probate court system. Utilizing this tool allows your family to maintain privacy and continuity during critical transitions. Each asset held within the trust remains fully accessible to you for daily needs and personal investments. This administrative framework supports your lifestyle while preparing a clear path for your heirs. The successful operation of this instrument depends entirely on complete funding and regular administrative maintenance. Understanding these functional boundaries ensures that your estate plan remains robust and effective under any circumstances.

> A basic revocable living trust is an administrative tool designed to bypass probate and manage assets, subject to statutory limits regarding taxes and personal creditor protection.

DOCUMENT SPOTLIGHT: TRUST CERTIFICATE

Purpose: To serve as a condensed document that confirms the trust's existence and identifies the trustee's administrative powers without revealing confidential details.

Key Authority: This certificate is accepted by financial institutions and county recorders to verify trustee authority during account updates and real estate transactions.

The Practical Capabilities of a Living Trust

A revocable living trust excels at managing and distributing family assets privately, avoiding the public oversight of the local probate court. By funding your trust with real estate, bank accounts, and investments, you ensure these assets transfer directly to your beneficiaries after your passing. This direct transfer saves your heirs from court fees, administrative delays, and public disclosure of family financial records.

The trust structure also provides exceptional protection during periods of physical or medical incapacity. Your designated successor trustee can step in immediately to manage your affairs, pay bills, and coordinate medical care without a court-appointed guardianship. This seamless continuation of authority preserves your personal autonomy and protects your family from stressful legal proceedings during a health emergency.

Emphasizing these primary benefits highlights the value of a well-funded trust in a complete estate plan. Securing this administrative continuity provides peace of mind, knowing that your personal affairs are organized and protected.

! **Common Mistake:** Believing that executing a revocable living trust agreement completes your plan, when in fact the trust remains empty and inactive until you formally retitle your assets.

The Limitations of a Revocable Trust Structure

A basic revocable living trust does not alter your personal tax obligations or shield your assets from personal creditor claims during your lifetime. All income generated by trust assets is taxed directly to you, and the assets remain accessible to satisfy any outstanding legal judgments.

Coordinating your revocable trust with other estate documents creates a cohesive protective framework for your family. Financial powers of attorney and medical directives address vital personal needs that fall outside trust authority. Keeping all beneficiary designations and asset titles aligned with your trust ensures the entire plan operates successfully.

STATE LAW REMINDER

"Estate and inheritance taxes are calculated based on the gross value of all property owned or controlled at death, including assets held in a revocable living trust."

Integrating a revocable trust with other complementary estate planning documents ensures that all areas of your life are protected. Working with an experienced professional helps you identify when specialized irrevocable structures or additional planning tools are required. Keeping your plan updated ensures that your legacy remains secure under current laws and family changes.

— KEY TAKEAWAY —

Probate Avoidance: Funded trusts transfer real estate and accounts privately to beneficiaries, bypassing court systems.

Tax Transparency: Revocable trusts are completely tax-neutral during life, requiring no separate tax identification numbers.

Funding Requirement: Retitling accounts, deeds, and investments remains essential to activate the trust's protective capabilities.

PART 3

Avoiding Probate

Focuses on probate avoidance, privacy, court delays, and how trust funding affects whether probate is truly avoided.

CHAPTER 13

Why Families Want to Avoid Probate

ORGANIZING AN ESTATE OFTEN INVOLVES finding ways to simplify the post-death transfer of family assets. Many individuals establish comprehensive plans specifically to bypass the formal administration procedures of local courts. This court-supervised process involves significant administrative steps that can affect the transition of family property. This legal arrangement serves to document your intentions in a thorough manner so that every detail remains perfectly preserved over time. By defining the administrative parameters in a clear instrument, you provide direct guidance for those who will handle your affairs in future years. Each designated individual receives a specific mandate to protect the integrity of the family estate according to the terms you outline. As a result of this meticulous planning, the structural alignment of the trust supports a seamless transition that benefits everyone involved. The formal settlement process can impose several systemic hurdles on families, making probate avoidance a primary goal of estate planning.

> Probate avoidance is the strategic organizing of assets during life to ensure their private, direct transfer to beneficiaries after death without court-supervised administration.

DOCUMENT SPOTLIGHT: PROBATE PETITION

Purpose: To formally request the local court to open estate administration and appoint a personal representative.

Key Authority: This filing initiates the court-supervised settlement process and begins the public notice period.

The Administrative Costs and Delays of Probate

The formal court settlement process involves several financial obligations, including court filing fees, publication costs, appraisal charges, and statutory executor fees. These combined expenses can reduce the total value of the estate available for distribution to your family. Along with financial costs, court-supervised administration requires mandatory waiting periods for creditor notifications and inventory filings. These structured intervals often extend the settlement process over several months, delaying access to assets for family members who may require immediate financial support.

The public nature of court filings means that estate records and asset inventories become matters of public record, accessible to anyone who requests them. This exposure can invite unwanted attention and compromise the financial privacy of the family during a sensitive time. Establishing a private transfer mechanism preserves your family's personal affairs from public disclosure.

> ! **Common Mistake:** Assuming that probate is a rapid administrative procedure, when in fact even simple uncontested estates often require many months of court coordination.

Court Supervision and Family Stress

Court-supervised administration requires the personal representative to seek judicial approval for many daily financial transactions, including selling real estate or distributing personal items. This continuous oversight can create administrative bottlenecks, requiring formal hearings and legal filings for standard decisions. The formal requirements of the court system can place an emotional burden on family members who must navigate complex legal paperwork while grieving.

Navigating these detailed procedural rules requires careful attention to avoid administrative delays and potential family disagreements. Working with experienced professionals ensures that all necessary filings comply with local statutes and court rules.

STATE LAW REMINDER

"Statutory probate fees and court-supervised timelines vary significantly by state, with some jurisdictions requiring mandatory formal accounting audits."

— KEY TAKEAWAY —

Financial Costs: Probate fees can reduce the total value of the estate available to beneficiaries.

Administrative Delays: Court-supervised timelines extend the asset transition period significantly.

Public Exposure: Court records are accessible to the public, compromising family financial privacy.

CHAPTER 14

Which Assets Go Through Probate?

UNDERSTANDING HOW ASSET OWNERSHIP AFFECTS the post-death transition is a fundamental part of estate planning. Different types of property are subject to distinct legal rules depending on how they are titled at the time of your passing. Assets held solely in an individual's name without any beneficiary designations represent the primary category of probate property. These individual holdings require formal court authorization before they can be legally transferred to heirs. Identifying these assets early allows you to organize your holdings in a structured and efficient manner. Selecting the appropriate legal title for your property ensures a smooth transfer of your family estate. The court-supervised process involves significant administrative steps that can affect the transition of family property. This systematic organization simplifies the eventual transition, allowing your personal representative to manage family property efficiently.

> Probate assets are individually owned properties that lack a surviving joint owner, trust funding, or valid beneficiary designation at the time of the owner's death.

DOCUMENT SPOTLIGHT: ASSET INVENTORY

Purpose: To list and value all solely owned property that must pass through the court-supervised probate process.

Key Authority: This inventory is submitted to the probate court to determine the size and value of the administered estate.

Individual Holdings and Real Estate

Real estate held solely in the name of an individual represents a common type of property that requires court-supervised probate administration. Financial accounts, including checking accounts, savings accounts, and investment portfolios that lack designated transfer-on-death arrangements, also fall under court authority. Personal property, such as vehicles, home furnishings, and personal belongings, must be formally cataloged and settled through the court system.

The personal representative must secure these individually owned assets, pay outstanding liabilities, and obtain court approval before transferring ownership to beneficiaries. This systematic process ensures that all legal claims against the estate are resolved before any property changes hands. Proper asset organization simplifies these administrative tasks and protects your family from unexpected delays.

Common Mistake: Believing that personal belongings and household items automatically transfer to family members without the need for court-supervised estate administration.

Business Interests and Probate Complexities

Sole proprietorships and closely held business interests without operational succession plans must also go through probate. The court-supervised process can disrupt business operations, as the personal representative must obtain judicial authority to manage accounts, pay employees, and conduct transactions. This administrative delay can impact the value of the business and complicate the eventual transfer to successors.

Organizing business holdings with formal transfer agreements ensures that company operations continue smoothly after your passing. Coordinating these business arrangements with your primary estate documents protects your commercial legacy and supports your partners.

STATE LAW REMINDER

"State statutes determine the threshold for small estates, allowing some low-value individually owned assets to bypass formal administration through simplified processes."

— KEY TAKEAWAY —

Individual Assets: Solely owned properties and accounts without beneficiary designations require court validation.

Real Estate: Individually titled land must be settled through court deeds before transfer.

Business Operations: Business interests without succession planning require judicial oversight to maintain operations.

CHAPTER 15

Which Assets Avoid Probate Automatically?

UTILIZING AUTOMATIC TRANSFER MECHANISMS represents an effective way to simplify the transition of family property. Many assets are structured to transfer directly to beneficiaries immediately upon the owner's passing, bypassing the court system entirely. This direct transition is governed by contract law and the specific terms of property deeds or financial agreements. Incorporating these automatic features into your estate plan secures your primary assets with minimal administrative effort. These arrangements support your financial goals while providing immediate protection for your family. Understanding how these default legal tools operate helps you build a resilient, coordinated plan. Relying on joint ownership is a practical way to manage shared household assets and primary residences. Preparing this complete administrative framework ensures your plan operates successfully when it is needed most.

> Non-probate assets are properties and accounts that transfer automatically to a surviving joint owner or named beneficiary by operation of law or contract.

DOCUMENT SPOTLIGHT: BENEFICIARY DESIGNATION

Purpose: To name specific individuals or entities who will receive the assets of an account directly upon the owner's death.

Key Authority: This contractual form overrides instructions in a will, ensuring a direct and private transfer of property.

Joint Tenancy and Rights of Survivorship

Real estate held in joint tenancy with right of survivorship transfers automatically to the surviving owner upon the passing of one co-owner. This legal transition occurs immediately, requiring only the filing of a certified death certificate and a simple affidavit with the county recorder. Financial accounts held jointly operate in a similar manner, giving the surviving account holder immediate, full access to the funds.

These automatic transfers provide continuous access to cash and property, protecting your family from administrative pauses during times of transition. Relying on joint ownership is a practical way to manage shared household assets and primary residences. Coordinating these titles with your overall estate goals ensures a harmonious and orderly transition.

!

Common Mistake: Assuming that joint ownership is always the best solution, when in fact adding a co-owner can expose your assets to their personal liabilities.

Contractual Beneficiary Arrangements

Financial contracts, such as life insurance policies, retirement accounts, and individual retirement annuities, utilize beneficiary designations to transfer assets directly to named heirs. Bank accounts can also feature payable-on-death designations, while investment accounts can utilize transfer-on-death arrangements to achieve a similar result. These designated assets transfer privately, bypass the probate court system, and remain unaffected by instructions in a Last Will and Testament.

Regular updating of beneficiary designations is essential to ensure that your financial assets transfer to your intended heirs. Keeping these contractual forms aligned with your personal relationships supports a secure and direct transition.

STATE LAW REMINDER

"Specific state statutes govern the validity of transfer-on-death deeds for real estate, requiring strict recording timelines with local land registries."

— KEY TAKEAWAY —

Joint Ownership: Properties held jointly transfer automatically to the surviving co-owner by operation of law.

Contractual Transfers: Beneficiary forms on insurance and retirement policies facilitate direct asset distribution.

POD/TOD Accounts: Payable-on-death designations provide immediate access to cash funds without court involvement.

CHAPTER 16

How a Living Trust Avoids Probate

ESTESTABLISHING A REVOCABLE LIVING TRUST provides a comprehensive method for managing and transferring family property outside the court system. This fiduciary entity holds legal title to your assets, removing them from your personal estate for probate administration purposes. Because the trust continues to exist after the grantor's passing, the assets remain under active, continuous management without interruption. This continuous structure allows the successor trustee to manage and distribute property privately according to your precise instructions. Utilizing a trust ensures that your family affairs remain completely confidential, protected from public disclosure. This systematic approach establishes a secure framework for preserving your personal and financial legacy. Trust administration occurs privately, allowing the successor trustee to complete the settlement process without public filings.

> A revocable living trust avoids probate by holding legal title to assets, permitting a successor trustee to manage and distribute those assets privately after the grantor's passing.

DOCUMENT SPOTLIGHT: TRUST DEED

Purpose: To formally transfer the ownership of a real estate property from an individual's personal name to the name of their living trust.

Key Authority: This recorded deed establishes the trust as the legal owner of the property, bypassing court administration.

The Continuity of Trust Ownership

The primary mechanism by which a revocable living trust avoids probate is the continuous ownership of its funded assets. When the grantor passes away, the trust itself remains active, and the successor trustee immediately assumes administrative authority over the property. Because the assets are owned by the trust entity rather than the individual, the probate court has no jurisdiction over them.

This administrative separation allows the successor trustee to manage investments, pay final bills, and distribute property to beneficiaries privately. The successor trustee acts in accordance with the specific terms outlined in the trust agreement, ensuring complete continuity. This structured arrangement protects your family from administrative delays and preserves your estate's value.

> **Common Mistake:** Believing that simply creating a trust agreement protects your assets from probate without completing the necessary asset transfers.

Private Administration and Asset Distribution

Trust administration occurs privately, allowing the successor trustee to complete the settlement process without public filings or court-supervised hearings. The trustee reviews the trust agreement, values the funded assets, satisfies valid estate debts, and distributes the remaining property directly to beneficiaries. This private process protects the family's financial details from public disclosure and prevents administrative delays.

Maintaining detailed administrative records ensures that the successor trustee can complete the distribution process efficiently and transparently. Proper documentation supports a smooth transition and maintains family harmony during a sensitive period of settlement.

STATE LAW REMINDER

"Trust administration must comply with state-specific fiduciary duties, which require the successor trustee to provide formal notice and accountings to beneficiaries."

— KEY TAKEAWAY —

Continuous Title: Assets held by the trust are not owned individually, keeping them outside probate jurisdiction.

Successor Management: Successor trustees assume control privately, maintaining administrative continuity.

Private Settlement: Trust distributions occur without public court filings, protecting family financial details.

CHAPTER 17

The Problem of an Unfunded Trust

DESIGNING A TRUST AGREEMENT IS A crucial first step, but the plan remains incomplete without systematic funding. An empty trust holds no assets, meaning that the entity cannot exercise authority over your property after your passing. Any assets left in your individual name at death remain subject to the court-supervised probate process. Formally transferring legal title of your assets to the trust is the essential step that activates its protective features. This funding process requires updating deeds, financial accounts, and beneficiary designations to align with your trust structure. Preparing this complete administrative framework ensures your plan operates successfully when it is needed most. An unfunded trust behaves like an empty vessel, possessing the structural capacity to hold assets but containing no actual property. Selecting the appropriate legal title for your property ensures a smooth transfer of your family estate.

> An unfunded trust is a trust agreement that has not been assigned legal title to any assets, rendering it inactive and unable to bypass probate for individually held property.

DOCUMENT SPOTLIGHT: FUNDING INSTRUCTIONS

Purpose: To provide a step-by-step guide for formally transferring real estate, financial accounts, and personal property to your living trust.

Key Authority: These instructions help the grantor align asset titles with the terms of the trust agreement.

The Consequences of an Empty Trust

An unfunded trust behaves like an empty vessel, possessing the structural capacity to hold assets but containing no actual property. If a grantor passes away with assets titled individually, those assets must be administered through the local probate court system. This administrative oversight can lead to the very delays, costs, and public disclosure that the trust was designed to avoid.

The successor trustee cannot manage or distribute property that remains titled in the grantor's individual name at the time of death. This separation can create administrative confusion and require court intervention to resolve asset ownership. Completing the funding process is essential to secure your estate plan and protect your heirs.

! **Common Mistake:** Assuming that signing a trust agreement automatically covers all your assets, when in fact each account and property deed must be formally retitled.

The Process of Trust Funding

Funding your trust involves formally changing the ownership of your primary assets from your individual name to the name of the trust. This process requires executing new deeds for real estate, retitling bank accounts, and updating beneficiary forms with financial institutions. Coordinating these changes ensures that all your valuable holdings remain under the authority of your trust agreement.

Regularly reviewing your asset titles ensures that newly acquired property is properly funded into your trust. Working with financial advisors and estate planning professionals helps you maintain complete organization and protects your family legacy.

STATE LAW REMINDER

"Real estate deeds must be recorded with local county offices to legally transfer ownership to a trust and bypass court-supervised estate administration."

— KEY TAKEAWAY —

Funding Requirement: Trusts only control assets that have been formally transferred into the name of the trust entity.

Probate Exposure: Individually owned assets left outside the trust must go through the court-supervised probate process.

Continuous Updates: Reviewing asset titles regularly ensures new holdings remain protected by the trust agreement.

PART 4

Deciding If a Living Trust Is Right for You

Helps readers evaluate whether they need a living trust based on family structure, property, privacy needs, and financial goals.

CHAPTER 18

When a Living Trust Makes Sense

EVALUATING PERSONAL CIRCUMSTANCES represents a fundamental step in determining the structural requirements of an estate plan. Many families decide to create a revocable living trust because they own real property, care for multiple beneficiaries, or prioritize financial privacy during transition periods. This proactive arrangement serves to document your intentions in a thorough manner so that every detail remains perfectly preserved over time. By defining the administrative parameters in a clear instrument, you provide direct guidance for those who will handle your affairs in future years. Each designated individual receives a specific mandate to protect the integrity of the family estate according to the terms you outline. As a result of this meticulous planning, the structural alignment of the trust supports a seamless transition that benefits everyone involved.

> A revocable living trust is highly appropriate for individuals who own real estate, have multiple heirs, value financial privacy, or wish to establish a structured plan for aging and potential incapacity.

DOCUMENT SPOTLIGHT: THE TRUST ANALYSIS

Purpose: To assess an individual's personal assets, family structure, and privacy goals to determine if a trust structure is beneficial.

Key Authority: This analysis guides the selection of estate planning tools by matching family needs with specific legal structures.

Homeownership and Complex Beneficiary Layouts

Real estate ownership represents a primary indicator that a living trust is a suitable planning tool for an estate. When an individual owns real property in more than one state, settling the estate through probate courts requires multiple court proceedings, a process known as ancillary probate. Establishing a single revocable trust allows all real estate holdings to be consolidated under one administrative umbrella, bypassing court actions in each individual state. This unified structure simplifies the responsibilities of the successor trustee and preserves the value of the estate for heirs.

Families with multiple beneficiaries or complex distribution goals also benefit from the structured nature of a trust agreement. The trust allows the grantor to specify when and how heirs receive their inheritances, protecting young beneficiaries from managing large sums of money prematurely. Trustees can hold assets in ongoing sub-trusts to cover educational costs, healthcare needs, and monthly living expenses over many years.

! **Common Mistake:** Assuming that a living trust is only necessary for exceptionally wealthy individuals, when in fact homeownership and simple privacy concerns are the actual drivers for choosing a trust.

Privacy Concerns and Planning for Longevity

Financial privacy remains a significant concern for families who wish to keep their asset details and distribution instructions confidential. Court-supervised probate proceedings are public, meaning that anyone can access estate inventories, beneficiary names, and distribution values. Utilizing a revocable living trust keeps these details entirely private, as the trust agreement is not filed with the court system. This administrative confidentiality shields your heirs from unwanted solicitations and protects your family's financial security.

STATE LAW REMINDER

"State statutes determine the legal definition of fiduciary capacity and outline the standard medical documentation required to activate a successor trustee's management authority."

Discussing these medical provisions with your successor trustee ensures a smooth and supportive transition when assistance is required. Establishing clear communication channels within the family prevents confusion and supports cooperative decision-making. This unified approach protects your personal interests and ensures that your chosen representatives feel completely prepared to help when needed.

KEY TAKEAWAY

Consolidated Assets: Trusts streamline the management of multiple properties and avoid out-of-state ancillary court actions.

Family Privacy: Administrative details remain confidential, preserving financial records from public court registries.

Aging Protection: Successor trustees step in privately to manage daily financial transactions during health transitions.

CHAPTER 19

When a Will May Be Enough

DETERMINING WHEN A SIMPLER PLANNING STRUCTURE is appropriate represents an important aspect of financial organization. For individuals with straightforward asset holdings and direct distribution goals, a Last Will and Testament can provide complete legal protection. This basic legal instrument allows you to designate an executor to settle outstanding liabilities and distribute remaining property to named heirs. Establishing this fundamental document ensures that your personal wishes are formally documented and legally recognized under state law. By appointing a trusted representative to manage this transition, you protect your estate from state-determined default distribution rules. As a result of this clear planning, your family can navigate the settlement process with reliable instructions and structured support.

> A Last Will and Testament is a suitable and efficient estate planning document for individuals with simple asset holdings, single-state properties, and direct, immediate distribution wishes.

DOCUMENT SPOTLIGHT: THE SIMPLE WILL

Purpose: To outline direct distribution instructions for solely owned assets and nominate executors and guardians for minor children.

Key Authority: This legal document is submitted to the local court after death to guide the supervised settlement of the estate.

Straightforward Estates and Small-Estate Processes

A will-based estate plan is highly functional for individuals who own a single primary residence and hold standard bank accounts with designated beneficiaries. When bank accounts, retirement funds, and life insurance policies feature valid beneficiary designations, these assets transfer automatically outside the court system. The remaining personal property, such as vehicles and household items, can be settled easily through the instructions in a simple will. This straightforward layout minimizes administrative costs and keeps the settlement process uncomplicated for your executor.

Many state jurisdictions offer simplified administration processes for estates that fall below a specific financial threshold, known as small-estate procedures. These streamlined options allow executors to settle estates using basic affidavits, bypassing the formal, lengthy court-supervised administration. Utilizing these small-estate shortcuts keeps the administrative burden minimal, making a trust structure unnecessary for smaller estates.

Common Mistake: Believing that a trust is always necessary to settle an estate, when in fact many jurisdictions offer fast-track legal processes for straightforward holdings.

Nomination of Guardians and Direct Distributions

For young families, the primary focus of an estate plan is often the nomination of guardians to care for minor children. A Last Will and Testament is the specific legal document used to designate these personal guardians, as trusts do not possess the legal capacity to nominate caregivers. This designation ensures that the court understands your wishes regarding child custody and personal care, protecting your family from custody disputes. Appointing these representatives in a will provides a secure foundation for your children's welfare.

STATE LAW REMINDER

"State regulations define the maximum financial limits for small-estate affidavit procedures and outline the specific witness requirements for executing a valid will."

Verifying these local financial thresholds ensures that your will-based plan operates successfully within your state's fast-track system. Regular reviews of your estate assets with a professional will help you confirm that your estate stays within these simplified limits over time. This ongoing attention allows your family to complete the settlement process with minimal administrative stress.

KEY TAKEAWAY

Direct Transfers: Wills provide a simple method for outright distributions to adult beneficiaries.

Guardian Nominations: The will remains the primary legal document for naming personal guardians for minor children.

Simplified Procedures: Small-estate affidavits allow lower-value estates to bypass formal, lengthy court administration.

CHAPTER 20

Living Trusts for Married Couples

COORDINATING PLANS FOR SPOUSES represents a critical part of securing long-term family stability. Married couples have unique property ownership patterns that require specialized planning structures to protect the surviving spouse and descendants. A revocable living trust can be established as a shared joint entity or as separate individual trusts depending on your asset mix and personal goals. Establishing this coordinate planning framework allows marital assets to be managed seamlessly through different stages of life. This unified approach serves to document your intentions in a thorough manner so that every detail remains perfectly preserved over time. As a result of this careful organization, the trust ensures that the surviving partner maintains continuous financial access and security.

> A marital trust plan utilizes joint or separate revocable trusts to manage shared and individual property, ensuring continuous support for the surviving spouse and clear inheritance paths for heirs.

DOCUMENT SPOTLIGHT: THE JOINT TRUST

Purpose: To hold and manage shared marital property within a single trust agreement created by both spouses.

Key Authority: This unified document authorizes the surviving spouse to continue managing the trust assets privately upon the passing of the partner.

Joint Trust Structures and Shared Property

A joint revocable living trust is a popular option for married couples who have been together for many years and hold their primary assets jointly. This shared structure holds the family home, joint bank accounts, and common investment portfolios under a single trust agreement. Both spouses serve as co-trustees, meaning they maintain equal, continuous control over the funded property during their lives. When one spouse passes away, the surviving partner assumes full administrative authority as the sole trustee, maintaining uninterrupted access to the marital assets.

This joint layout simplifies ongoing trust administration, as the couple continues to manage their financial affairs through a single entity. The assets remain protected from court-supervised probate processes, protecting the surviving spouse from administrative interruptions during a sensitive time. This continuous access ensures that household bills, medical expenses, and daily costs are covered without delay.

Common Mistake: Assuming that a joint trust is suitable for every couple, when in fact separate trusts are highly beneficial for blended families with independent heirs.

Separate Trusts and Blended Family Planning

Establishing separate individual trusts is a highly effective strategy for couples in blended families or those who possess significant independent assets. Each spouse creates an independent trust agreement to hold their personal property, separate bank accounts, and individual real estate holdings. This separate structure allows each partner to determine the precise inheritance paths for their respective beneficiaries, such as children from previous relationships. Coordinating these separate trusts ensures that the surviving partner is supported while protecting the long-term inheritance of descendants.

STATE LAW REMINDER

"State marital property regulations govern the classification of shared and separate assets, requiring careful alignment with your trust funding strategies."

Aligning your trust funding with these local marital laws ensures that your property distributions remain fully compliant and secure. Understanding how local property classifications apply to your shared assets helps you make informed choices during the funding process. This careful alignment provides a clear and harmonious path forward that respects the rights of each family member.

KEY TAKEAWAY

Continuous Marital Access: Joint trusts provide the surviving spouse with immediate, private access to shared marital assets.

Separate Protection: Separate trusts allow spouses in blended families to protect the inheritances of their respective children.

Structured Support: Sub-trusts can hold marital property to support the surviving spouse while preserving the long-term family legacy.

CHAPTER 21

Living Trusts for Single People

PLANNING FOR PERSONAL SECURITY remains a vital responsibility for single adults who want to protect their welfare and assets. Establishing a revocable living trust provides a reliable platform for managing property during your lifetime and after your passing. This protective framework allows you to appoint trusted individuals to handle your financial affairs and medical decisions if you experience an emergency. By outlining these instructions in a clear agreement, you provide direct guidance for those who will assist you in future years. Each designated helper receives a specific mandate to act in your best interest, maintaining complete administrative clarity. As a result of this careful organization, the trust ensures that your personal autonomy is protected under any circumstances. The everyday coordination of your assets remains entirely within your personal preview, providing uninterrupted access to your holdings. This reliable operational layout ensures that the transition to a trust structure supports your ongoing lifestyle and long-term security goals.

> A revocable living trust is highly appropriate for single individuals who wish to select trusted helpers, manage asset distributions privately, and establish clear protective structures for potential incapacity.

DOCUMENT SPOTLIGHT: HEALER DESIGNATION

Purpose: To appoint specific individuals to manage your financial accounts and coordinate personal care if you experience a medical emergency.

Key Authority: This designation provides the successor trustee with immediate authority to handle bills and make investments during transitions.

The Selection of Fiduciary Representatives

Selecting a successor trustee is a crucial decision for single individuals establishing a living trust. The successor trustee must possess the practical skills and personal reliability necessary to manage your investments, pay bills, and handle administrative affairs. Many grantors choose a professional fiduciary, such as a trust department or a licensed advisor, to ensure objective and systematic management. This professional selection protects your assets from administrative errors and ensures that all trust terms are executed with complete fidelity.

Establishing these fiduciary relationships early in life provides a secure foundation for your personal security. Taking the time to discuss your goals with your designated representative prepares them to assist you effectively.

Common Mistake: Delaying the appointment of a successor trustee under the assumption that a single adult does not require structured support during their lifetime.

Securing Assets and Organizing Distributions

A revocable living trust allows a single individual to designate exactly how their estate will be distributed after their passing. The trust agreement can outline outright transfers or structured distributions to family members, friends, or charitable organizations. This customized approach ensures that your assets are used in accordance with your personal values and long-term intentions. The successor trustee manages the distribution process privately, avoiding the public oversight and delays of local probate courts.

STATE LAW REMINDER

"State statutory default rules determine the distribution of assets for single individuals who pass away without a valid estate plan, often directing property to distant relatives."

Verifying these local statutory rules ensures that your trust agreement operates successfully within your state's legal system. Regular reviews of your estate assets with a professional will help you confirm that your plan stays compliant with current regulations over time. This proactive approach protects your personal interests and ensures that your chosen representatives can fulfill their duties with complete legal authority.

KEY TAKEAWAY

Trusted Helpers: Appointing successor trustees ensures that reliable individuals manage your affairs during health transitions.

Incapacity Protection: Living trusts bypass court-appointed guardianship, preserving your personal independence.

Asset Control: Outlining direct distributions ensures that your property is transferred in accordance with your values.

CHAPTER 22

Living Trusts for Parents with Minor Children

SECURING THE FUTURE WELFARE OF MINOR CHILDREN represents a primary concern for parents who are organizing an estate plan. Establishing a comprehensive planning structure allows you to protect your children's financial security and designate trusted personal caregivers. This proactive arrangement serves to document your intentions in a thorough manner so that every detail remains perfectly preserved over time. By defining the administrative parameters in a clear instrument, you provide direct guidance for those who will handle your affairs in future years. Each designated individual receives a specific mandate to protect the integrity of the family estate according to the terms you outline. As a result of this meticulous planning, the structural alignment of the trust supports a seamless transition that benefits everyone involved. The everyday coordination of your assets remains entirely within your personal preview, providing uninterrupted access to your holdings. This reliable operational layout ensures that the transition to a trust structure supports your ongoing lifestyle and long-term security goals.

> A marital trust plan for parents utilizes a living trust to coordinate inheritances for young children while incorporating a Last Will and Testament to nominate legal guardians.

DOCUMENT SPOTLIGHT: CHILD'S TRUST

Purpose: To hold and manage shared inheritance funds for the benefit of minor children until they reach designated milestones.

Key Authority: This trust agreement authorizes the trustee to distribute funds privately for the children's education, health, and support.

Structuring Financial Inheritances for Young Heirs

Managing inheritances for minor children requires a structured and protective approach to secure their long-term financial stability. A living trust allows parents to appoint a trustee to manage inheritance funds, make investments, and distribute assets according to specific instructions. The trustee can release funds periodically for educational costs, health needs, and daily living expenses as the child grows. This ongoing administration ensures that young heirs are supported while protecting them from managing large sums of money prematurely.

The structure of the trust provides clear guidelines that help the trustee manage the assets responsibly. This careful organization provides comfort to parents, knowing that their children's financial future is fully secured.

!

Common Mistake: Believing that a living trust can legally designate a personal guardian for minor children, when only a Last Will and Testament can perform this function.

Naming Guardians and Coordinating Estate Documents

A comprehensive estate plan for parents requires coordinating a revocable living trust with a Last Will and Testament. The revocable living trust manages financial assets privately, and the Last Will and Testament acts to designate personal guardians for minor children. Appointing these personal representatives in a will provides a secure foundation for your children's welfare and daily care. This coordinate planning ensures that both financial management and personal care are fully organized in the event of an emergency.

Coordinating these documents protects your family from custody challenges and legal disputes. Reviewing these designations regularly ensures that your choices remain aligned with your family's needs and current relationships.

STATE LAW REMINDER

"State regulations require a valid Last Will and Testament to formally designate legal guardians for minor children."

Verifying these local guardianship rules ensures that your child's future care is secure under your state's legal system. Regular reviews of your designated guardians with an estate professional help confirm that your choices remain aligned with current criteria. This proactive alignment protects your family's welfare and establishes complete clarity within your estate plan.

KEY TAKEAWAY

Financial Oversight: Trusts manage child inheritances responsibly, distributing funds for educational and healthcare needs.

Guardian Nominations: Last Wills and Testaments remain the only legal instruments capable of naming personal guardians.

Coordinated Planning: Aligning wills and trusts secures both the physical care and financial future of minor children.

CHAPTER 23

Living Trusts for Blended Families

NAVIGATING THE ESTATE PLANNING REQUIREMENTS of a blended family requires a structured and balanced approach to protect all family members. Married partners in blended families often have unique property ownership patterns that require specialized planning structures to protect a surviving spouse and descendants from previous relationships. Establishing this coordinate planning framework allows marital assets to be managed seamlessly through different stages of life. This unified approach serves to document your intentions in a thorough manner so that every detail remains perfectly preserved over time. As a result of this careful organization, the trust ensures that the surviving partner maintains continuous financial access and security. By defining these parameters clearly, you provide direct guidance for those who will handle your estate in future years. Each designated individual receives a specific mandate to protect the integrity of the family assets according to the terms you outline. The everyday coordination of your assets remains entirely within your personal preview, providing uninterrupted access to your holdings.

> A revocable trust plan for blended families utilizes structured provisions to secure support for the surviving spouse while guaranteeing the long-term inheritance of children from previous relationships.

DOCUMENT SPOTLIGHT: FAMILY SUB-TRUST

Purpose: To hold and manage a grantor's assets within a separate sub-trust to support the spouse while preserving the principal for children.

Key Authority: This trust agreement authorizes the trustee to distribute income to the spouse while guaranteeing the final transfer to the grantor's heirs.

Balancing Spousal Support and Descendants' Inheritances

Married partners in blended families often face unique planning needs when balancing spousal support with child inheritances. A revocable living trust can be structured to hold assets in an ongoing sub-trust to support the surviving spouse during their lifetime. This arrangement ensures the surviving partner maintains financial comfort and continuous access to marital property. Upon the spouse's passing, the remaining trust principal transfers directly to the grantor's designated children from a previous relationship.

This balanced approach provides a fair and structured solution that respects the needs of all family members. Appointing an independent trustee to manage these funds ensures that distributions are made objectively and in accordance with your instructions.

Common Mistake: Relying on simple joint wills that leave all assets to the surviving spouse, as the surviving partner can legally change terms and disinherit stepchildren.

Reducing Administrative Friction and Family Conflict

Utilizing structured trusts helps blended families minimize administrative friction and protect long-term family harmony. Outlining clear instructions in the trust agreement reduces the potential for misunderstandings between a surviving spouse and children from previous relationships. The trustee acts as an objective manager, distributing assets precisely according to the terms set by the original grantor. This methodical administration secures the family legacy and provides complete clarity for all beneficiaries.

STATE LAW REMINDER

"State marital property regulations govern the classification of shared and separate assets, requiring careful alignment with your trust funding strategies."

Aligning your trust funding with local marital property regulations ensures that your estate plans remain fully compliant and secure. Consulting with experienced estate professionals helps you structure your trust to prevent potential disputes among family members. This careful alignment provides a clear and harmonious path forward that respects the rights of each family member.

KEY TAKEAWAY

Balanced Distribution: Trusts can provide lifetime support for a spouse while securing the inheritance of biological children.

Friction Reduction: Outlining precise administrative rules prevents family misunderstandings during the settlement process.

Independent Management: Utilizing professional trustees ensures objective and fair execution of trust instructions.

CHAPTER 24

Living Trusts for Unmarried Couples

CREATING A COMPREHENSIVE ESTATE PLAN for unmarried partners represents an important aspect of financial organization and mutual protection. Unmarried couples have unique legal profiles, as statutory default laws do not automatically provide inheritance or decision-making rights to partners. Establishing a revocable living trust allows partners to designate trusted helpers, manage shared properties, and secure mutual financial support privately. This proactive arrangement serves to document your intentions in a thorough manner so that every detail remains perfectly preserved over time. By defining the administrative parameters in a clear instrument, you provide direct guidance for those who will handle your affairs in future years. Each designated individual receives a specific mandate to protect the integrity of the family estate according to the terms you outline. As a result of this meticulous planning, the structural alignment of the trust supports a seamless transition that benefits everyone involved. The everyday coordination of your assets remains entirely within your personal preview, providing uninterrupted access to your holdings.

> An estate plan for unmarried partners uses a living trust and explicit legal directives to establish mutual inheritance rights and decision-making authority not provided by law.

DOCUMENT SPOTLIGHT: PARTNER AGREEMENT

Purpose: To outline shared property agreements and document mutual financial intentions within a single, coordinated estate plan.

Key Authority: This agreement provides clear evidence of partner consent, supporting the legal transfer of trust-held assets.

Establishing Legal Protections and Property Rights

Unmarried couples require explicit legal planning to secure property rights and inheritance protections for each other. Because state statutory default laws do not automatically recognize unmarried partners, formal legal documents are necessary to establish these transitions. A revocable living trust allows partners to title shared properties, bank accounts, and investments in the name of the trust. This joint administration ensures that the surviving partner maintains continuous and private access to shared assets after a partner's passing.

Using the trust to hold shared assets protects both partners from sudden loss of access to bank accounts or real estate holdings. This structured layout establishes a secure and reliable framework that protects your shared financial security.

! **Common Mistake:** Believing that a long-term relationship automatically grants marital property rights or default inheritance protections under state intestacy laws.

Designing Medical and Financial Directives

In addition to a living trust, unmarried couples should execute comprehensive medical and financial directives. These complementary documents grant partners the legal authority to make critical decisions during health emergencies. Appointing your partner as a financial agent and healthcare proxy protects their ability to assist you when needed most. This coordinate planning ensures that both financial assets and personal welfare are fully protected under all circumstances.

Regularly updating these medical directives keeps your plans aligned with your current relationship status and personal choices. Discussing these arrangements with your partner ensures that you both feel prepared to manage decisions during challenging transitions.

STATE LAW REMINDER

"State default statutes do not recognize unmarried partners for hospital visitation, medical decisions, or automatic asset inheritance."

Verifying these default statutory limitations ensures that your partner is fully protected under your local legal system. Regular updates to your healthcare proxies and financial powers of attorney keep your designations aligned with current family needs. This active management provides a secure framework that protects your partner's welfare and maintains family clarity.

KEY TAKEAWAY

Explicit Protections: Unmarried partners must use written trusts to establish property rights and inheritance protections.

Asset Access: Holding shared assets within a living trust ensures the surviving partner maintains continuous financial access.

Medical Authority: Executing health proxies grants unmarried partners the legal capacity to make medical decisions.

PART 5

Creating the Trust

Explains the key decisions readers must make before setting up a living trust.

CHAPTER 25

Choosing the Grantor, Trustee, and Successor

SELECTING KEY DECISION-MAKERS forms the foundational step in establishing a functional and resilient estate plan. The alignment of these core roles determines the efficiency of daily asset management and the integrity of future property transitions. Grantors must carefully evaluate the personal qualifications, availability, and willingness of those they nominate to serve as trustees. Appointing individuals who possess a strong sense of responsibility and financial administrative skills supports the stable execution of your long-term intentions. This protective planning provides your family with a clear path forward, securing your assets and ensuring your instructions are followed with complete fidelity. The everyday coordination of your assets remains entirely within your personal preview, providing uninterrupted access to your holdings. This reliable operational layout ensures that the transition to a trust structure supports your ongoing lifestyle and long-term security goals.

> A comprehensive trust plan requires defining the specific roles of the grantor, trustee, and successor trustee to ensure continuous and responsible management of the estate.

DOCUMENT SPOTLIGHT: FIDUCIARY APPOINTMENT

Purpose: To formally designate the initial and successor trustees who will manage and distribute the trust assets.

Key Authority: This legal section defines the precise operational powers and limitations of the appointed fiduciaries.

Defining the Primary Operational Roles

The grantor establishes the trust structure and defines the guidelines for managing all funded assets. During the grantor's lifetime, they typically serve as the initial trustee to maintain complete, continuous control over banking transactions, investments, and real property. This dual capacity keeps asset management straightforward, allowing you to buy, sell, or modify property with standard ease. The trustee holds legal title to the trust assets, managing them solely for the benefit of the designated participants.

Serving as a trustee involves a high standard of care and loyalty, requiring the representative to manage assets with complete honesty and transparency. The trustee must keep accurate accounting records, file fiduciary tax returns, and protect the estate from financial loss. This continuous responsibility ensures that the grantor's original intentions are executed with complete fidelity.

Common Mistake: Assuming that a trustee must be a family member, when in fact professional trustees or corporate trust departments often provide more objective and stable financial management.

Selecting Qualified Successor Trustees

Selecting a successor trustee requires evaluating the representative's long-term availability, administrative skills, and personal integrity. The successor trustee assumes active management only upon the death, resignation, or incapacity of the initial trustee, acting privately without court supervision. Appointing an alternate successor trustee ensures administrative continuity if your primary choice is unable or unwilling to serve. This proactive planning protects your assets and provides your family with reliable guidance during transitions.

STATE LAW REMINDER

"State statutory rules outline the legal qualifications for fiduciaries, including age requirements and clean background standards."

Consulting with an experienced estate planning professional ensures your fiduciary selections comply fully with local standards. This careful planning protects your family from administrative challenges and ensures a harmonious transition of wealth.

KEY TAKEAWAY

The Grantor: Establishes the trust and retains complete authority to manage or modify the agreement during life.

The Trustee: Manages the funded assets in accordance with the strict fiduciary guidelines defined in the trust.

Successor Selection: Choosing capable alternate trustees ensures uninterrupted asset management during future transitions.

CHAPTER 26

Choosing Beneficiaries

IDENTIFYING THE INDIVIDUALS AND ORGANIZATIONS who will eventually inherit your assets is a deeply personal and significant aspect of estate planning. Grantors must clearly define who will receive the benefits of the trust property, establishing a structured path for the transition of wealth. This deliberate selection ensures that your accumulated assets are passed to your intended loved ones, supporting their financial needs and securing their future. Appointing primary and backup beneficiaries creates a resilient framework that adapts to changes in family circumstances and personal relationships. Each designated participant receives a specific inheritance in accordance with your precise instructions, maintaining complete administrative clarity. This systematic organization simplifies the transition, allowing the successor trustee to manage distributions efficiently and harmoniously. The everyday coordination of your assets remains entirely within your personal preview, providing uninterrupted access to your holdings. This reliable operational layout ensures that the transition to a trust structure supports your ongoing lifestyle and long-term security goals.

> Choosing beneficiaries involves designating the specific primary and backup heirs who will inherit the trust property, ensuring an orderly transition of family wealth.

DOCUMENT SPOTLIGHT: THE BENEFICIARY SCHEDULE

Purpose: To list the designated heirs and specify the percentages or specific assets each participant will receive after the grantor's passing.

Key Authority: This contractual schedule guides the successor trustee in distributing trust property privately and directly to the heirs.

Establishing Primary and Contingent Designations

Primary beneficiaries are the first individuals or organizations designated to inherit trust assets upon the grantor's passing. To ensure the estate plan remains robust, grantors must also name contingent or backup beneficiaries who will receive the assets if the primary heirs pass away before the trust is distributed. This protective layering ensures that your assets are always transferred according to your wishes, preventing estate property from passing under default state laws.

Providing complete legal names, current contact information, and relationships for each beneficiary helps the successor trustee locate heirs quickly. This clear documentation minimizes administrative delays and ensures that distributions proceed smoothly. The successor trustee uses this detailed schedule to execute transfers privately, protecting the family's financial security.

> **Common Mistake:** Naming minor children as direct beneficiaries of a trust or insurance policy, which can trigger court-appointed guardianships and administrative delays.

Addressing Percentages and Specific Legacy Gifts

Grantors can distribute inheritances by assigning specific percentages of the total estate or designating specific dollar amounts and tangible items. Assigning percentages allows the inheritance to scale naturally with changes in the overall value of your trust portfolio. Specific gifts, such as family heirlooms or fixed monetary sums, are distributed first, with the remaining balance divided among the primary beneficiaries. This structured distribution method ensures complete fairness and helps prevent misunderstandings among family members.

STATE LAW REMINDER

"State statutory notice laws require successor trustees to formally notify all qualified beneficiaries and heirs when a trust administration begins."

Fulfilling these notice requirements ensures complete transparency and protects the successor trustee from potential administrative disputes. Working with an experienced professional helps you maintain full compliance with all local estate notification guidelines.

KEY TAKEAWAY

Primary Heirs: Receive the initial allocation of trust assets according to the timelines set by the grantor.

Contingent Backup: Protects the estate plan by designating alternate beneficiaries in case of unexpected family changes.

Scale with Percentages: Utilizing percentage-based distributions allows inheritances to adapt naturally to changes in estate value.

CHAPTER 27

Deciding Who Gets What

ALLOCATING PERSONAL PROPERTY AND FINANCIAL HOLDINGS requires a thoughtful approach to balance family harmony with practical asset management. Grantors must decide how to divide their estate, considering both the monetary value of assets and the sentimental importance of family heirlooms. This process involves cataloging valuable belongings, real estate, and investment portfolios to create a clear plan for their eventual distribution. Outlining these instructions in a comprehensive trust agreement prevents misunderstandings among heirs and ensures your legacy is preserved. Appointing a successor trustee to manage this division ensures that your personal property is distributed in an orderly and respectful manner. This methodical coordination supports your family during a sensitive period of transition, providing complete clarity for all participants. The everyday coordination of your assets remains entirely within your personal preview, providing uninterrupted access to your holdings. This reliable operational layout ensures that the transition to a trust structure supports your ongoing lifestyle and long-term security goals.

> Deciding who gets what involves organizing the division of financial assets, real estate, and sentimental property to promote family harmony and execute your wishes.

DOCUMENT SPOTLIGHT: PROPERTY MEMORANDUM

Purpose: To compile a detailed, separate list of personal belongings and heirlooms and specify which heirs will receive them.

Key Authority: This written memorandum is incorporated into the trust agreement, allowing the grantor to update personal gifts easily.

Allocating Sentimental Property and Heirlooms

Dividing sentimental property, such as family photos, jewelry, and heirlooms, can be one of the most challenging aspects of estate administration. Grantors can prevent emotional disputes among heirs by utilizing a personal property memorandum to designate specific items for specific individuals. This informal list can be updated at any time during your lifetime without requiring a formal amendment to the primary trust agreement.

Discussing these sentimental allocations with family members helps you understand their personal preferences and expectations. This open communication ensures that your choices are respected and reduces the likelihood of disagreements during the transition period. The successor trustee uses this detailed list to distribute personal items directly and privately to your loved ones.

Common Mistake: Assuming that family members will easily agree on the division of sentimental items, when in fact these belongings can trigger deep emotional disputes.

Balancing Equal and Unequal Allocations

Determining the division of financial assets requires deciding between equal distributions among children or customized allocations based on individual needs. Grantors can use their trust to provide unequal distributions to support a beneficiary with special medical needs or educational goals. If you decide to make unequal allocations, explaining your reasoning in the trust document or a separate letter can help family members understand your intentions and accept the distribution layout.

STATE LAW REMINDER

"State statutory rules govern the legal validity of separate personal property memorandums, requiring specific signature and reference protocols."

Aligning your property memorandum with local execution standards ensures that your personal property designations are legally recognized. This careful preparation provides your family with a clear and reliable guide for dividing sentimental items.

KEY TAKEAWAY

Sentimental Items: Utilizing separate property memorandums helps organize the distribution of personal heirlooms privately.

Open Communication: Discussing personal belongings with family members prevents emotional disputes and aligns expectations.

Distribution Strategy: Defining the reasons for unequal financial allocations promotes understanding and harmony among heirs.

CHAPTER 28

Planning for Young Beneficiaries

STRUCTURING INHERITANCES FOR YOUNG HEIRS requires a protective and strategic approach to ensure their financial security and encourage responsible stewardship. Passing substantial assets directly to a young adult who lacks financial experience can lead to rapid depletion of the funds and long-term administrative challenges. Establishing a dedicated sub-trust within your revocable living trust allows you to appoint a capable trustee to manage inheritance funds on their behalf. The trustee holds and invests the assets, distributing funds for the child's essential needs according to your precise instructions. This continuous oversight protects the young beneficiary while helping them build the skills needed for mature asset management. This coordinated framework provides your family with absolute clarity, ensuring that your wealth supports your children's development. The everyday coordination of your assets remains entirely within your personal preview, providing uninterrupted access to your holdings. This reliable operational layout ensures that the transition to a trust structure supports your ongoing lifestyle and long-term security goals.

Planning for young beneficiaries involves utilizing ongoing sub-trusts to manage inheritances, distributing funds for educational and healthcare needs until designated age milestones are met.

DOCUMENT SPOTLIGHT: THE SUB-TRUST PROVISION

Purpose: To create a distinct, ongoing sub-trust that holds and manages shared inheritance assets for the benefit of minor heirs.

Key Authority: This provision authorizes the trustee to manage investment accounts and distribute funds for the children's essential needs.

Designing Age-Based Distribution Milestones

A revocable living trust allows parents to establish a structured timeline for distributing assets to young beneficiaries. To ensure responsible distribution, the trust can hold the assets and distribute them gradually at designated age milestones, such as twenty-five, thirty, and thirty-five. This phased release allows young adults to gain financial experience, manage smaller sums of money first, and build long-term stability.

During this holding period, the trustee retains complete authority to manage the trust assets and make investments on behalf of the beneficiaries. This professional oversight ensures that the inheritance is protected from market volatility and inflation, preserving its value for the future. Phased distributions align with your children's development, supporting their financial maturity over many years.

Common Mistake: Distributing a substantial inheritance outright to a young adult at age eighteen, which can lead to rapid depletion of the funds and financial instability.

FUNDING ESSENTIAL EDUCATIONAL AND HEALTHCARE NEEDS

While the trust holds the principal assets, the trustee can distribute funds continuously to cover the beneficiary's essential educational, healthcare, and daily living expenses. This flexible access ensures that your children have the resources needed to pursue college degrees, technical training, and necessary medical care. The trustee evaluates each request in accordance with the standards defined in the trust agreement, ensuring the funds are used responsibly.

STATE LAW REMINDER

"State statutory fiduciary standards govern how trustees manage and invest trust assets held for the long-term benefit of minor beneficiaries."

Ensuring that your trustee complies with these local fiduciary standards protects the inheritance from mismanagement and legal challenges. This careful structure guarantees that your wealth continues to support your children's development with complete safety.

KEY TAKEAWAY

Phased Releases: Distributing inheritances gradually at specific age milestones encourages long-term financial responsibility.

Essential Support: Trustees can distribute trust funds continuously to cover educational costs, healthcare, and daily living needs.

Professional Oversight: Appointing a capable trustee protects inheritance assets from market volatility and premature depletion.

CHAPTER 29

Special Instructions for Difficult Situations

ADDRESSING THE UNIQUE CHALLENGES OF VULNERABLE HEIRS requires a highly protective and structured estate planning framework to secure their welfare and preserve family assets. Some beneficiaries face persistent financial difficulties, such as substantial personal debt, divorce risks, or challenges with poor money management. Grantors must design their trust agreements to shield inheritance funds from these external threats, ensuring that support remains continuous and secure. Incorporating spendthrift provisions and discretionary trust structures allows you to appoint an independent trustee to manage and distribute property on behalf of the beneficiary. This professional administration protects the estate principal from being seized by creditors or depleted rapidly due to administrative errors. This methodical approach secures your legacy, providing a stable foundation that protects your family under any circumstances. The everyday coordination of your assets remains entirely within your personal preview, providing uninterrupted access to your holdings. This reliable operational layout ensures that the transition to a trust structure supports your ongoing lifestyle and long-term security goals.

> Special instructions for difficult situations involve utilizing spendthrift provisions and discretionary sub-trusts to protect inheritance funds from a beneficiary's personal debt, divorce, or financial mismanagement.

DOCUMENT SPOTLIGHT: SPENDTHRIFT PROVISION

Purpose: To establish a protective sub-trust that prevents a beneficiary from selling, pledging, or assigning their interest in the inheritance.

Key Authority: This provision authorizes the trustee to distribute funds directly to service providers, protecting the assets from creditor claims.

Implementing Spendthrift and Discretionary Protections

A spendthrift trust provision is a highly effective tool for protecting inheritances from a beneficiary's personal creditors and potential lawsuit judgments. This clause prevents the beneficiary from transferring their future trust distributions to third parties, ensuring the assets remain under the authority of the independent trustee. Creditors cannot seize assets held within the trust because the beneficiary does not possess direct ownership or control over the property.

The independent trustee can make payments directly to service providers, landlords, and educational institutions on behalf of the beneficiary, bypassing the participant entirely. This discretionary distribution method ensures that the beneficiary's essential needs, such as housing and healthcare, are met while keeping the remaining principal safe. This protective layout preserves the estate from rapid depletion, supporting the beneficiary's welfare over their lifetime.

(!) **Common Mistake:** Leaving an outright, unrestricted inheritance to a beneficiary facing active creditor lawsuits or severe financial management challenges.

Supporting Beneficiaries with Special Needs

Providing support for a beneficiary with physical or cognitive challenges requires utilizing a specialized special needs trust structure. This distinct sub-trust holds and manages assets to cover supplemental needs, such as personal care, therapy, and specialized equipment, without affecting the beneficiary's eligibility for government assistance programs. The trustee coordinates all distributions to ensure compliance with strict public benefit guidelines, protecting the participant's essential supportive network.

STATE LAW REMINDER

"State statutory rules govern the legal validity of spendthrift provisions, requiring specific execution language and administrative boundaries."

Aligning your spendthrift provisions with these local legal standards guarantees that your assets remain secure from external creditor claims. This proactive coordination protects your family's financial security and ensures that your heirs receive continuous and safe support.

KEY TAKEAWAY

Spendthrift Protection: Spendthrift clauses prevent creditors from seizing inheritance assets held within the protective trust structure.

Direct Distributions: Trustees can pay expenses directly to service providers to ensure the beneficiary's essential needs are met.

Special Needs Planning: Utilizing dedicated special needs trusts preserves eligibility for government assistance while funding supplemental care.

PART 6

Funding the Living Trust

Explains how to transfer assets into the trust so the trust actually works.

CHAPTER 30

What It Means to Fund a Trust

THE FORMAL PROCESS OF TRUST FUNDING represents the physical transfer of personal assets into the legal ownership of the trust entity. This crucial administrative transition is what gives the trust agreement its practical validity and allows it to protect your assets. A signed trust document remains empty and inactive until you systematically change the titles of your bank accounts, deeds, and investments. Funding your trust ensures that your primary assets are held securely, prepared to bypass the probate court system privately after your passing. Preparing this complete administrative framework secures your legacy and provides continuous support for your loved ones. The everyday coordination of your assets remains entirely within your personal preview, providing uninterrupted access to your holdings. This reliable operational layout ensures that the transition to a trust structure supports your ongoing lifestyle and long-term security goals.

> Trust funding is the process of transferring the legal ownership of your personal assets, including real estate, bank accounts, and investments, into the name of the trust entity.

DOCUMENT SPOTLIGHT: THE FUNDING CHECKLIST

Purpose: To serve as a comprehensive inventory of all personal assets that must be formally retitled.

Key Authority: This checklist helps the grantor track the progress of deeds, accounts, and beneficiary updates.

THE ESSENTIAL NATURE OF ASSET TRANSFER

Trust funding is a systematic process that requires changing the owner of record on each asset from your individual name to the name of the trust. Financial institutions and local county recording offices require specific documentation to complete these ownership updates. The trustee must present a trust certificate or the complete trust agreement to verify their administrative authority. Completing these transfers ensures that the trust governs the assets privately, avoiding any future court-supervised probate proceedings.

Taking the time to understand these administrative steps helps you organize your financial holdings in a highly systematic manner. Providing the correct documentation to each institution ensures that your ownership records are updated without unnecessary delay. This proactive preparation protects your family from future administrative challenges during transitions. Maintaining complete organization throughout this funding phase establishes a secure foundation for your overall estate plan.

Common Mistake: Believing that listing your assets on the trust's schedule of assets is sufficient to transfer ownership without formally retitling each individual account.

Managing Newly Acquired Property

Maintaining a fully funded trust requires regular reviews of your asset titles as you acquire new property over time. Any newly purchased real estate, investment accounts, or bank funds must be titled in the name of the trust at the time of purchase. This ongoing coordination ensures that your estate plan remains complete and effective under all circumstances. Properly aligning these titles protects your assets and keeps your family's transition private and straightforward.

STATE LAW REMINDER

"State statutes govern the specific registration requirements for funding different asset classes into a revocable trust."

Reviewing these registration requirements with a qualified professional confirms that each asset is funded correctly. This careful coordination ensures that your entire estate plan operates with complete reliability when needed. Taking these structured steps protects your accumulated wealth and establishes a resilient baseline for your family. This systematic completion of your funding checklist provides lasting peace of mind for everyone.

KEY TAKEAWAY

Ownership Update: Trusts only control assets that have been formally retitled into the name of the trust entity.

Continuous Reviews: Titling newly acquired property in the trust's name maintains complete planning protection.

Probate Avoidance: Properly funded assets transfer privately to your beneficiaries, bypassing court systems.

CHAPTER 31

Transferring Real Estate into the Trust

FORMALLY TRANSFERRING REAL ESTATE into the name of your revocable trust represents one of the most significant steps in funding your estate plan. Real property left in an individual's name must go through the public probate court system, causing unnecessary delays and costs for your heirs. Conveying your primary residence or land holdings to the trust preserves these valuable assets from court-supervised administration. This transition requires executing and recording a new deed with the local county land registry office. Properly aligning your property titles with your trust agreement secures your home and simplifies the future transition of your estate. The everyday coordination of your assets remains entirely within your personal preview, providing uninterrupted access to your holdings. This reliable operational layout ensures that the transition to a trust structure supports your ongoing lifestyle and long-term security goals.

> Real estate funding is the process of conveying land and residential properties from individual ownership to the trust entity using a formally recorded deed.

DOCUMENT SPOTLIGHT: THE QUITCLAIM DEED

Purpose: To formally convey real property from an individual's personal name to the name of their revocable trust.

Key Authority: This recorded document establishes the trust as the legal owner of the property for probate avoidance.

Executing and Recording the Property Deed

Transferring real estate requires preparing a new deed, such as a quitclaim deed or a warranty deed, to convey ownership to the trust. This deed must be signed by the grantor, formally notarized, and recorded with the local county land registry where the property is located. Recording the deed provides public notice that the trust is the legal owner of the property, bypassing court administration. This systematic process ensures that the property transfers privately and directly to your beneficiaries after your passing.

Recording the property deed promptly ensures that your real estate remains fully secure under the terms of the trust agreement. This simple administrative action establishes a clear public record of ownership to support a seamless transition. Working closely with local county recorders helps you complete the conveyance process in complete accordance with local guidelines. This methodical approach preserves your home and provides your loved ones with absolute clarity regarding the family estate.

Common Mistake: Neglecting to record the executed property deed with the local county recorder, leaving the transfer legally incomplete.

Mortgages and Homeowners Insurance

Conveying a home to a revocable living trust preserves existing mortgage loans and maintains stable terms under federal protection guidelines. Grantors must also notify their homeowners insurance provider and title insurance company to add the trust as an additional insured party. This simple administrative update ensures that your insurance coverage remains fully active and protects the trust assets from liabilities. Coordinating these notifications secures your real property and maintains continuous coverage for your home.

STATE LAW REMINDER

"Local jurisdictions regulate property tax exemptions and require specific transfer tax affidavit filings when conveying real property to a trust."

Filing these required affidavits with the county assessor prevents any disruption to your primary residence tax exemptions. This proactive step guarantees that your property transfer remains fully compliant with local tax codes. Successfully recording your deeds preserves your primary residential benefits while securing your long-term legacy. This coordinate planning shields your home from unnecessary court proceedings and ensures stable administration.

KEY TAKEAWAY

Deed Recording: Property transfers require a signed and recorded deed to be recognized as legally complete.

Insurance Coordination: Adding the trust as an additional insured party protects the assets from liability.

Tax Exemptions: Submitting county tax affidavits preserves valuable primary residence tax exemptions.

CHAPTER 32

Bank Accounts and Brokerage Accounts

RETITLING FINANCIAL HOLDINGS into your revocable living trust represents an essential part of funding your estate plan. Checking accounts, savings accounts, and investment portfolios held individually are subject to court-supervised probate administration after your passing. Transferring these accounts into the trust ensures that your funds remain continuously accessible to you during life and to your successor trustee during transitions. This process involves contacting your financial institutions and submitting updated signature cards and a trust certificate. Coordinating these bank and brokerage transfers secures your cash assets and simplifies the daily management of your estate. The everyday coordination of your assets remains entirely within your personal preview, providing uninterrupted access to your holdings. This reliable operational layout ensures that the transition to a trust structure supports your ongoing lifestyle and long-term security goals.

> Account retitling is the administrative process of updating the official ownership records of bank and investment accounts to reflect the trust as the legal owner.

DOCUMENT SPOTLIGHT: THE CERTIFICATE OF TRUST

Purpose: To serve as a condensed summary of the trust agreement that confirms the trustee's authority without revealing confidential details.

Key Authority: This certificate is accepted by financial institutions to update account titles and verify administrative powers.

The Process of Account Retitling

Funding cash and investment holdings requires changing the official account ownership from your individual name to the name of the trust. Financial institutions require a copy of your trust certificate, updated signature cards, and specific funding applications to complete this transition. The bank assigns the trust accounts under your personal social security number, keeping your annual income tax filing straightforward and unchanged. This unified structure ensures that your daily check-writing, deposit activities, and investment transactions proceed without any disruption.

Cooperating with your banking representatives ensures that your checking and savings accounts are updated with complete accuracy. Preparing the required trust certificates in advance allows the institution to process your request without procedural delays. This detailed coordination maintains your continuous access to cash reserves for daily expenses and personal goals. Establishing this secure financial baseline protects your liquid assets and simplifies ongoing administrative oversight.

! **Common Mistake:** Assuming that simply listing bank accounts on the trust's schedule of assets is sufficient to transfer ownership without contacting the financial institution.

Brokerage Accounts and Shared Investments

Retitling brokerage accounts and mutual funds requires coordinating with your investment custodians to execute new transfer agreements. These institutions update the account registration to reflect the trustee's legal ownership while maintaining your existing investment holdings and portfolio strategies. This continuous management protects your financial assets from market interruptions and preserves their long-term growth. Properly aligning these investment titles ensures that your successor trustee can manage the portfolio privately during periods of incapacity.

STATE LAW REMINDER

"Banking regulations require financial institutions to verify the identity of all trustees and successor trustees under federal compliance standards."

Providing the required identification and trust documentation promptly prevents administrative delays during the account transition. This careful organization secures your liquid assets and ensures your financial accounts remain continuously funded. Maintaining updated records with your financial custodians guarantees that cash reserves remain fully accessible under all circumstances. This systematic alignment ensures that your daily banking needs are continuously supported with complete safety.

KEY TAKEAWAY

Direct Custody: Financial institutions must officially update account registrations to fund bank assets into the trust.

Tax Transparency: Trust-held bank accounts utilize the grantor's social security number, maintaining simple tax filing.

Ongoing Access: Properly funded investment accounts remain fully accessible to you and your successor trustee.

CHAPTER 33

Retirement Accounts and Living Trusts

MANAGING RETIREMENT ASSETS requires a specialized planning approach due to the unique tax rules governing these accounts. Individual retirement arrangements and employer-sponsored plans are structured differently than standard bank accounts or real property. These tax-deferred holdings remain titled in your individual name during your lifetime. Attempting to transfer ownership of a retirement plan directly to a trust triggers immediate income tax liabilities and penalties. Coordinating these accounts requires utilizing contractual beneficiary designations to ensure a smooth, tax-efficient transfer of funds to your heirs. The everyday coordination of your assets remains entirely within your personal preview, providing uninterrupted access to your holdings. This reliable operational layout ensures that the transition to a trust structure supports your ongoing lifestyle and long-term security goals.

> Retirement account coordination is the process of utilizing beneficiary designations to transfer individual retirement assets directly to heirs, preserving tax-deferred status.

DOCUMENT SPOTLIGHT: BENEFICIARY FORM

Purpose: To formally designate the primary and contingent beneficiaries who will inherit your retirement assets directly upon your passing.

Key Authority: This recorded contractual form overrides instructions in a will, bypassing court-supervised administration privately.

The Mechanism of Beneficiary Transfers

Retirement accounts transfer directly to named beneficiaries by operation of contract, completely bypassing the local probate court system. To secure these funds, you must submit updated beneficiary designation forms to each retirement plan custodian. Naming primary and contingent beneficiaries on these forms ensures that your retirement assets are transferred privately and directly according to your wishes. This contractual transition preserves the tax-deferred status of the accounts, protecting your beneficiaries from unnecessary tax burdens.

Aligning your retirement designations with your primary planning goals requires careful coordination with each account custodian. Submitting updated beneficiary forms ensures that these valuable savings transfer directly and privately to your heirs. This methodical approach secures your financial legacy while preserving the tax-deferred growth of your accumulated funds. Taking these protective steps early provides your family with clear instructions and immediate financial security.

!

Common Mistake: Attempting to retitle a retirement account into the name of a revocable living trust, triggering immediate taxes and early withdrawal penalties.

Coordinating Trusts as Retirement Beneficiaries

Grantors can designate their revocable living trust as a secondary or primary beneficiary of retirement accounts under specific planning circumstances. This arrangement is highly useful when providing for minor children or beneficiaries who require structured financial oversight. The trustee receives the retirement distributions and manages them according to the rules outlined in the trust agreement, ensuring responsible stewardship. Working with an experienced professional helps you structure these designations to comply with federal tax guidelines.

STATE LAW REMINDER

"Internal Revenue Service regulations determine the mandatory distribution timelines and tax treatment for inherited retirement accounts."

Aligning your beneficiary designations with current federal tax codes protects your heirs from accelerated tax obligations. This careful coordination ensures that your retirement savings are preserved and distributed in a highly efficient manner. Seeking professional guidance helps you navigate these complex federal tax rules to maximize the value of your savings. This thorough preparation ensures that your hard-earned assets provide lasting support for future generations.

KEY TAKEAWAY

Contractual Transfer: Retirement assets bypass probate entirely through the use of valid beneficiary designations.

Individual Title: Accounts remain in the individual owner's name during life to preserve tax-deferred status.

Trust Options: Naming the trust as a backup beneficiary provides structured management of retirement funds for heirs.

CHAPTER 34

Life Insurance and Beneficiary Designations

COORDINATING LIFE INSURANCE PROCEEDS represents a highly effective way to provide immediate financial support for your family. Life insurance policies are contractual agreements that transfer death benefits directly to named beneficiaries outside the court system. This private transfer occurs rapidly, providing heirs with the cash needed to cover final expenses, debts, and administrative costs. While these policies operate automatically, aligning their beneficiary designations with your overall estate plan is essential for complete protection. Utilizing these insurance features secures your family's welfare and establishes a reliable foundation for their future. The everyday coordination of your assets remains entirely within your personal preview, providing uninterrupted access to your holdings. This reliable operational layout ensures that the transition to a trust structure supports your ongoing lifestyle and long-term security goals.

> Life insurance coordination is the process of aligning policy beneficiary forms with your estate plan to ensure the direct, private transfer of death benefits to your loved ones.

DOCUMENT SPOTLIGHT: POLICY DESIGNATION

Purpose: To formally designate the primary and contingent beneficiaries who will receive the insurance death benefits.

Key Authority: This completed contract form guides the insurance company in distributing proceeds privately and directly.

The Role of Direct Contractual Transfers

Life insurance proceeds transfer directly to named beneficiaries by operation of contract, bypassing the public probate court system entirely. This direct distribution allows the insurance company to pay the death benefit quickly, often within a few weeks of receiving the certified death certificate. These funds remain private, protecting your family's financial details from public disclosure and court costs. Coordinating these policy designations with your personal relationships supports a secure and direct transition of wealth.

Coordinating your insurance policies with your overall estate goals provides a strong protective shield for your family. Ensuring that all beneficiary designations are complete and accurate allows the insurance company to process claims efficiently. This proactive organization guarantees that immediate cash resources are available to cover final family needs. Maintaining this continuous alignment protects your loved ones and supports long-term financial stability.

! **Common Mistake:** Failing to name contingent beneficiaries on a life insurance policy, which can cause the proceeds to default to your probate estate if primary heirs pass away.

Naming the Trust as Policy Beneficiary

Naming your revocable living trust as the beneficiary of your life insurance policy is a highly effective strategy for young families. This arrangement allows the insurance proceeds to flow directly into the trust, where the successor trustee manages and invests the funds for minor children. The trustee distributes the money gradually for the children's education, healthcare, and daily living needs according to your instructions. This structured transition provides a secure layer of protection, ensuring your family is cared for responsibly.

STATE LAW REMINDER

"State statutes govern the claims of personal creditors against life insurance proceeds, often providing strong protections for named beneficiaries."

Verifying these local creditor protections ensures that your insurance distributions remain fully secure from external liabilities. This careful planning protects your family's financial future and provides complete peace of mind. Coordinating these policy designations with your core estate plan establishes a resilient financial safety net for your loved ones. This orderly transition of assets guarantees that immediate cash resources are available during sensitive family times.

KEY TAKEAWAY

Rapid Benefits: Life insurance proceeds transfer directly to named beneficiaries privately and outside probate.

Contingent Protection: Naming alternate beneficiaries prevents policy benefits from defaulting to a probate estate.

Trust Coordination: Designating the trust as beneficiary provides structured, professional management of funds for heirs.

◇ PART 7 ◇

Documents That Support a Living Trust

Shows why a trust alone is not a complete estate plan and explains the documents that work with it.

CHAPTER 35

The Pour-Over Will

EXECUTING A POUR-OVER WILL represents an important safety measure in a complete estate plan. This specialized legal document is designed to work in coordination with your revocable living trust. It ensures that any assets held in your individual name at the time of your passing are automatically directed into your trust. This process consolidates your estate under a single administrative structure, protecting your family from disorganized transitions. Having this backup mechanism in place secures your assets and supports an orderly distribution process. Each designated individual receives a specific mandate to protect the integrity of the family estate according to the terms you outline. As a result of this meticulous planning, the structural alignment of the trust supports a seamless transition that benefits everyone involved. The everyday coordination of your assets remains entirely within your personal preview, providing uninterrupted access to your holdings. This reliable operational layout ensures that the transition to a trust structure supports your ongoing lifestyle and long-term security goals.

> A pour-over will is a specific type of will that directs the probate court to transfer any individually held assets into an existing revocable living trust upon the creator's passing.

DOCUMENT SPOTLIGHT: THE POUR-OVER WILL

Purpose: To serve as a safety device that automatically captures any assets held in an individual's name at death and transfers them into an existing revocable living trust structure.

Key Authority: This specialized will directs the probate court to distribute any individually held property to the trustee of the trust, ensuring a unified asset distribution process.

The Practical Operation of a Safety Device

A pour-over will acts as an essential safety net, protecting your estate plan from omissions and newly acquired property under individual ownership. If you pass away owning assets individually, this will directs the probate court to distribute those assets directly to your successor trustee. This transfer integrates the property into your existing trust, allowing it to be managed and distributed according to your original instructions. Utilizing this coordinate structure ensures that all your valuable holdings are unified under a single plan.

Coordinating these legal instruments ensures that every individually owned asset remains fully within your planned distribution framework. The executor named in the will coordinates closely with the successor trustee to manage these transfers. This careful alignment provides your family with a clear and unified path for settling your estate. Organizing these documents in a systematic manner protects your family from administrative confusion.

Common Mistake: Assuming that a pour-over will avoids the probate process entirely, when assets passing under this will require court-supervised probate before transfer to the trust.

The Legal Path of Estate Consolidation

The court-supervised process for assets passing under a pour-over will involves standard filing requirements and notice provisions. The executor named in the will must present the document to the local probate court to validate its terms. Once validated, the court authorizes the transfer of the individually held property to the trustee of your living trust. This legal transition ensures that all outstanding debts are satisfied before the assets are merged into the trust.

STATE LAW REMINDER

"State regulations govern the validation of pour-over wills and determine the specific court procedures required to transfer assets to a trustee."

Verifying these local financial limits helps you structure your estate plan to utilize the most efficient transfer methods available. Regular consultations with an estate professional ensure that your will and trust remain fully compliant with current state standards. Organizing your assets in this manner protects your family from administrative gaps and ensures complete stability. This careful coordination ensures that your hard-earned assets are preserved for future generations with complete safety.

KEY TAKEAWAY

Estate Integration: Pour-over wills capture individually held assets and transfer them to your living trust.

Court Validation: Assets passing under this will must be validated by the local probate court.

Unified Planning: Coordinating wills and trusts ensures all property is distributed under a single plan.

CHAPTER 36

Durable Financial Power of Attorney

AUTHORIZING A DESIGNATED REPRESENTATIVE to manage your financial affairs is an essential part of preparing for potential health transitions. A durable financial power of attorney is a formal legal document that grants a trusted individual the authority to act on your behalf if you become incapacitated. This protective arrangement ensures that your bills are paid, your investments are managed, and your business transactions proceed without any disruption. By outlining these instructions in a clear agreement, you provide direct guidance for those who will assist you in future years. Each designated agent receives a specific mandate to act solely in your best interest, maintaining complete administrative clarity. As a result of this careful organization, the document ensures that your personal affairs are protected under any circumstances. The everyday coordination of your assets remains entirely within your personal preview, providing uninterrupted access to your holdings. This reliable operational layout ensures that the transition to a trust structure supports your ongoing lifestyle and long-term security goals.

> A durable financial power of attorney is a legal document that authorizes a trusted representative to manage your banking, real estate, and business affairs if you become unable to do so.

DOCUMENT SPOTLIGHT: FINANCIAL POWER OF ATTORNEY

Purpose: To authorize a designated representative to manage banking transactions, sign tax returns, and conduct business affairs on your behalf during periods of physical or medical incapacity.

Key Authority: This document remains legally valid and active if the creator experiences temporary or permanent medical incapacity, preventing court-appointed guardianship.

The Selection of a Financial Agent

Choosing a financial agent requires evaluating the representative's practical skills, personal reliability, and understanding of financial management. The agent should be someone who is fully prepared to handle administrative tasks, banking transactions, and business decisions responsibly. This selection protects your personal assets and ensures that your daily financial routine is maintained with complete integrity. Discussing your goals with your designated representative ensures they understand their fiduciary obligations and act in accordance with your wishes.

Selecting a highly responsible representative ensures that your daily financial affairs are managed with the utmost care and transparency. The agent must maintain meticulous records of all transactions to demonstrate complete fiduciary accountability. This direct communication with financial institutions allows your household needs to be met during emergencies. Organizing this document in a systematic manner provides your family with a clear and reliable path.

(!) **Common Mistake:** Assuming that a financial power of attorney remains valid after the creator passes away, when all authority granted under this document terminates immediately at death.

Managing Financial Affairs and Asset Protection

The agent's authority can cover a wide range of financial transactions, including managing bank accounts, executing tax filings, and paying residential expenses. This comprehensive access allows your representative to keep your household running smoothly during a medical emergency. The agent must maintain detailed records of all transactions to demonstrate complete transparency and fiduciary responsibility. Properly aligning this document with your living trust ensures that all assets are managed cohesively.

STATE LAW REMINDER

"State statutes govern the formatting, witness requirements, and notary protocols necessary to execute a valid durable financial power of attorney."

Verifying these local signature requirements ensures that your power of attorney remains fully valid and accepted by major banks. This careful preparation prevents administrative delays when your agent needs to act on your behalf during health emergencies. Establishing these safeguards ensures that your financial interests are managed with complete safety and continuity. This thorough planning protects your accumulated wealth and supports your loved ones with complete clarity.

KEY TAKEAWAY

Immediate Authority: Financial agents can manage accounts and pay bills during periods of incapacity.

Fiduciary Duty: Appointed representatives must act solely in your best interest, maintaining detailed records.

Formal Validation: Power of attorney documents require specific signatures, witnesses, and notarization.

CHAPTER 37

Health Care Power of Attorney

DESIGNATING A TRUSTED HEALTHCARE REPRESENTATIVE is a fundamental step in securing your medical autonomy during critical health transitions. A health care power of attorney, also known as a healthcare proxy, allows you to name a trusted individual to make medical choices for you if you cannot speak for yourself. This protective arrangement ensures that your personal values, ethical beliefs, and treatment preferences are fully respected by medical professionals. By outlining these instructions in a clear agreement, you provide direct guidance for those who will make decisions during challenging times. Each designated representative receives a specific mandate to protect your bodily autonomy, maintaining complete clarity. As a result of this careful organization, the document ensures that your physical welfare is protected under any circumstances. The everyday coordination of your assets remains entirely within your personal preview, providing uninterrupted access to your holdings. This reliable operational layout ensures that the transition to a trust structure supports your ongoing lifestyle and long-term security goals.

> A health care power of attorney is a legal document that designates a trusted representative to make medical decisions on your behalf if you are unable to communicate your wishes.

DOCUMENT SPOTLIGHT: HEALTH CARE PROXY

Purpose: To authorize a designated healthcare representative to make medical treatment decisions on your behalf if you become temporarily or permanently incapacitated.

Key Authority: This document provides physicians and hospitals with clear directions regarding who has the legal capacity to consent to or decline medical treatments.

Selecting a Compassionate Healthcare Representative

Choosing a healthcare representative requires selecting an individual who understands your personal values and is prepared to advocate for your medical preferences. The representative must possess the personal strength to make difficult decisions under stressful circumstances, ensuring your wishes are followed. This selection protects your bodily autonomy and ensures that your medical treatment remains aligned with your ethical beliefs. Discussing your healthcare goals with your representative ensures they are fully prepared to act on your behalf with complete confidence.

Discussing your medical values and preferences with your representative prepares them to act on your behalf with complete confidence. This open communication ensures that your advocate can make difficult decisions under stressful circumstances in accordance with your wishes. The designated representative coordinates directly with medical staff to ensure you receive appropriate and compassionate care. Organizing this document in a systematic manner provides your loved ones with absolute clarity.

Common Mistake: Assuming that close family members can automatically make medical decisions without a formal health care power of attorney, which can lead to administrative delays and family disputes.

Coordinating Medical Directives and Living Wills

A complete healthcare plan coordinates a health care power of attorney with a living will to provide comprehensive guidance. The health care power of attorney designates the decision-maker, and the living will specifies your preferences regarding life-prolonging treatments. This combined approach ensures that your medical representatives have a clear road map to guide their choices. The successor trustee can coordinate with your healthcare agent to fund necessary treatments from the trust assets.

STATE LAW REMINDER

"State statutory rules define the legal requirements for executing healthcare directives, including mandatory signature witnesses and specific formatting standards."

Ensuring your medical documents meet these local standards guarantees that hospitals and emergency personnel will recognize your agent's authority. This proactive planning protects your bodily autonomy and supports your family during challenging transitions. This deliberate arrangement shields you from unexpected court interventions and supports family harmony during health emergencies. Establishing these protective directives completes your comprehensive estate plan with complete safety and security.

KEY TAKEAWAY

Medical Autonomy: Health proxies authorize trusted representatives to make medical choices when you cannot communicate.

Comprehensive Planning: Coordinating health proxies with living wills provides complete guidance for medical care.

Legal Validation: Healthcare directives require specific signatures, witnesses, and notary seals to be recognized.

CHAPTER 38

Living Will and Advance Directive

DOCUMENTING PERSONAL HEALTHCARE PREFERENCES provides a secure and reliable platform for guiding medical decisions during critical situations. This proactive process involves the creation of an advance directive that outlines your specific choices regarding medical care. Having these instructions formally recorded ensures that your personal values and beliefs are fully respected by physicians. By defining these parameters in a clear instrument, you provide direct guidance for those who will oversee your physical welfare. Each designated instruction receives a specific mandate to support the preservation of your personal dignity and care. As a result of this meticulous planning, the structural alignment of the directive supports a seamless transition that benefits everyone involved. The everyday coordination of your assets remains entirely within your personal preview, providing uninterrupted access to your holdings. This reliable operational layout ensures that the transition to a trust structure supports your ongoing lifestyle and long-term security goals.

> A living will is a formal legal document that outlines an individual's specific instructions regarding medical treatments and life-sustaining procedures during critical health situations.

DOCUMENT SPOTLIGHT: THE LIVING WILL

Purpose: To outline specific instructions regarding medical care and treatment preferences during emergencies.

Key Authority: This document provides physicians and family members with legally binding guidance when you cannot communicate.

Establishing Clear Medical Preferences

Writing down your specific healthcare preferences ensures that medical professionals can administer care in complete accordance with your wishes. This documentation provides clear guidelines regarding the use of specialized medical equipment, cardiac support, and other clinical procedures. Appointing a healthcare representative to communicate these instructions ensures that your physical welfare remains fully protected during emergencies. Having these explicit directions prepared in advance removes the burden of difficult decision-making from your family members.

Discussing these clinical choices with your family members promotes complete understanding of your personal intentions. This open dialogue ensures that your representatives feel completely supported when carrying out their duties. You can also share copy documents with your primary physicians to update your medical records. Organizing these files in a systematic manner protects your personal interest and ensures compliance.

Common Mistake: Assuming that a living will only applies to permanent conditions, when in fact it can guide temporary treatment plans during acute medical emergencies.

Integrating Healthcare Directives with Estate Plans

Coordinating medical directives with your primary estate documents creates a cohesive protective framework for your personal welfare. The healthcare representative works in alignment with your financial agents to ensure that medical costs are managed responsibly. This systematic arrangement protects your personal autonomy while securing the continuous administration of your household affairs. Proper organization of these health documents ensures that your personal preferences are respected under all circumstances.

STATE LAW REMINDER

"State statutes govern the specific formatting, witness signatures, and mandatory disclosure statements required to execute a legally binding living will."

Verifying these local signature rules ensures that your healthcare directives are recognized as legally valid by local medical centers. This active coordination protects your bodily autonomy and supports your designated representatives during critical transitions. Regularly reviewing your medical documents with a qualified advisor ensures they remain fully compliant with current state regulations. This thorough preparation provides a secure framework that protects your personal welfare under all circumstances.

KEY TAKEAWAY

Medical Autonomy: Living wills provide clear, written instructions regarding your specific medical treatment preferences.

Family Clarity: Explicit directives remove the emotional burden of decision-making from family members during emergencies.

Legal Compliance: Ensuring your documents comply with local signature rules guarantees their immediate acceptance by hospitals.

CHAPTER 39

HIPAA Authorization

SECURING THE CONTINUOUS PROTECTION of personal health information represents a fundamental aspect of comprehensive estate planning. This process involves executing a formal authorization that complies with federal privacy standards to permit trusted individuals access to your medical files. Having this document in place ensures that your named representatives can coordinate with medical professionals during sensitive situations. By defining these access parameters in a clear instrument, you provide direct guidance for those who will support your care. Each designated individual receives a specific mandate to obtain clinical updates and coordinate treatment plans according to your instructions. As a result of this meticulous planning, the structural alignment of the authorization supports a seamless transition that benefits everyone involved. The everyday coordination of your assets remains entirely within your personal preview, providing uninterrupted access to your holdings. This reliable operational layout ensures that the transition to a trust structure supports your ongoing lifestyle and long-term security goals.

> A HIPAA authorization is a formal legal document that grants healthcare providers permission to share an individual's protected health information with designated representatives.

DOCUMENT SPOTLIGHT: THE HIPAA RELEASE

Purpose: To authorize healthcare providers to release confidential medical information to named family members or representatives.

Key Authority: This release form ensures that your designated helpers can obtain medical records and discuss treatment plans with doctors.

The Practical Necessity of Medical Privacy Waivers

Federal privacy laws protect individual medical histories, meaning that healthcare providers cannot disclose clinical details to family members without explicit written consent. Executing a formal HIPAA authorization allows your designated helpers to discuss your condition with attending physicians during health emergencies. This immediate access to information allows your representatives to make informed choices regarding your treatment and care plans. Providing this written waiver removes administrative barriers and supports a smooth coordination process with medical staff.

Providing your designated representatives with this authorization allows them to obtain medical updates directly from doctors. This formal release form acts in coordination with your healthcare proxy to ensure complete information access. You can specify which medical files can be disclosed and identify any limitations you wish to establish. Maintaining this clear documentation prevents administrative delays and supports your family during health transitions.

Common Mistake: Believing that holding a medical power of attorney automatically grants access to medical records, when hospitals often require a distinct HIPAA release.

Coordinating Information Access with Fiduciary Roles

Aligning medical privacy waivers with your financial powers of attorney ensures complete administrative continuity during health transitions. Your financial agent requires access to medical billing records to settle outstanding insurance claims and coordinate payments. This seamless flow of information allows your fiduciaries to manage your household accounts with complete transparency. Proper coordination of these documents protects your estate from administrative bottlenecks and unnecessary delays.

STATE LAW REMINDER

"Federal regulations outline strict guidelines for protected health information, requiring medical release forms to contain specific disclosure language."

Verifying these local and federal release standards ensures that your authorization document is immediately accepted by healthcare networks. This active coordination protects your personal privacy and supports your chosen advocates during difficult transitions. Regularly updating your list of authorized representatives ensures your medical files remain accessible only to trusted helpers. This thorough preparation provides a secure framework that protects your personal welfare under all circumstances.

KEY TAKEAWAY

Privacy Protection: Federal regulations shield medical records from unauthorized access, requiring explicit written consent for disclosure.

Immediate Access: HIPAA waivers grant designated helpers the legal right to obtain updates and discuss treatment with physicians.

Fiduciary Alignment: Coordinating releases with financial agents ensures seamless management of billing and insurance affairs.

CHAPTER 40

Letter of Instruction

ASSEMBLING A PRACTICAL GUIDE is an invaluable way to simplify the overall administration of your estate. This process involves the creation of a detailed letter of instruction that outlines the locations of vital records and personal preferences. Having these details compiled in a single document ensures that your family can manage daily tasks without unnecessary confusion. By defining these parameters in a clear instrument, you provide direct guidance for those who will handle your affairs. Each designated helper receives a specific mandate to locate financial accounts, notify contacts, and honor your personal wishes. As a result of this meticulous planning, the structural alignment of the letter supports a seamless transition that benefits everyone involved. The everyday coordination of your assets remains entirely within your personal preview, providing uninterrupted access to your holdings. This reliable operational layout ensures that the transition to a trust structure supports your ongoing lifestyle and long-term security goals.

> A letter of instruction is an informal estate planning document that provides representatives with practical guidance regarding account locations, contacts, personal wishes, and care plans.

DOCUMENT SPOTLIGHT: THE MEMORANDUM

Purpose: To compile practical, non-technical details regarding the daily administration of your personal and financial affairs.

Key Authority: This letter guides your executor and successor trustee in locating important accounts, contacts, and personal records.

Providing Actionable Details for Your Family

A letter of instruction provides a centralized directory of your bank accounts, investment portfolios, and insurance policies. This document also outlines specific instructions for the care of your pets, including their dietary needs and preferred veterinary clinics. Listing the contact information for your estate planning professionals, financial advisors, and close relatives simplifies the notification process. This practical guide ensures that your representatives can manage daily administrative responsibilities with complete confidence.

Providing this structured outline ensures that your family has access to critical financial files during transitions. Your chosen helper can coordinate directly with professionals using the detailed contact sheets you provide. This direct access to accounts saves your representatives from searching through extensive paper archives. Maintaining this document in an accessible location provides immediate guidance when assistance is required.

(!) **Common Mistake:** Assuming that a letter of instruction is a legally binding substitute for a will or trust, when it is actually an informal helper document.

Documenting Personal Messages and Final Wishes

The letter of instruction also provides a personal space for documenting your specific preferences regarding memorial services and final arrangements. Writing down these wishes helps your family coordinate ceremonies in complete accordance with your personal values. This document can also contain personal messages and expressions of gratitude to be delivered to your loved ones. This thoughtful compilation supports family harmony and provides immediate, practical directions during a sensitive transition.

STATE LAW REMINDER

"A letter of instruction operates as an informal guide, serving as an essential reference to assist fiduciaries during estate settlement."

Verifying local custom and probate guidelines helps you organize your letter to support the formal administration of your estate. This active coordination protects your personal preferences and ensures that your chosen helpers feel completely supported during their duties. Regularly reviewing and updating your account lists and contact details keeps your letter fully accurate over time. This thorough preparation provides a secure framework that protects your personal welfare under all circumstances.

KEY TAKEAWAY

Practical Inventory: Letters of instruction list the locations of bank accounts, deeds, insurance policies, and digital records.

Personal Directions: Outlining preferences for memorial services and pet care provides immediate guidance for your family.

Family Harmony: Centralizing contact lists and personal messages reduces administrative confusion during sensitive transitions.

CHAPTER 41

Digital Asset Planning

ORGANIZING YOUR MODERN ESTATE requires extending your planning efforts to encompass your entire digital footprint and online presence. This process involves identifying all online accounts, cloud storage files, and digital properties that you own or manage. Having these digital assets organized ensures that your personal photographs, creative works, and financial records remain secure. By defining these parameters in a clear instrument, you provide direct guidance for those who will access these systems. Each designated representative receives a specific mandate to manage or preserve your online data according to your instructions. As a result of this meticulous planning, the structural alignment of your digital plan supports a seamless transition that benefits everyone involved. The everyday coordination of your assets remains entirely within your personal preview, providing uninterrupted access to your holdings. This reliable operational layout ensures that the transition to a trust structure supports your ongoing lifestyle and long-term security goals.

> Digital asset planning is the process of identifying, securing, and organizing instructions for the management and transfer of online accounts and digital property.

DOCUMENT SPOTLIGHT: DIGITAL INVENTORY

Purpose: To catalog all online accounts, passwords, cloud storage locations, and digital assets in a single secure record.

Key Authority: This directory guides your designated representatives in accessing, managing, or closing your online accounts.

Cataloging and Securing Online Accounts

A complete digital estate plan begins with a thorough inventory of your email accounts, financial portals, and cloud subscriptions. Utilizing a secure password manager or encrypted file ensures that your designated representative can access these systems when needed. This organized access protects valuable digital property, including personal photographs, creative writings, and domain registries, from permanent loss. Providing clear instructions for each account ensures that your digital legacy is managed in accordance with your wishes.

Coordinating this modern checklist ensures that your family can retrieve valuable photographs and personal journals. Your designated representatives can also manage digital subscriptions and shut down inactive online portals. This active oversight protects your private accounts from security risks and unauthorized use. Organizing these credentials within a unified estate plan ensures complete safety for your legacy.

! **Common Mistake:** Sharing passwords on a written list in your will, which becomes a public document when admitted to court for probate administration.

Coordinating Digital Access with Fiduciary Powers

Authorizing your representatives to manage your digital assets requires updating your primary estate planning documents with explicit digital access provisions. These legal clauses grant your executor and successor trustee the authority to interact with online service providers on your behalf. This coordination prevents service disruptions, secures valuable accounts, and ensures the orderly closure of digital properties. Properly aligning these legal powers protects your privacy and preserves your digital legacy for future generations.

STATE LAW REMINDER

"State statutes and the federal Revised Uniform Fiduciary Access to Digital Assets Act govern how executors and trustees legally interact with online providers."

Verifying these state statutory standards ensures that your digital access clauses are fully recognized by major online platform providers. This active coordination protects your personal data and supports your chosen representatives during critical administrative transitions. Regularly updating your digital inventory keeps your password records and account lists fully accurate as your digital footprint grows. This thorough preparation provides a secure framework that protects your personal welfare under all circumstances.

KEY TAKEAWAY

Digital Inventory: Cataloging online accounts, financial portals, and cloud subscriptions prevents permanent asset loss.

Explicit Authority: Adding digital access clauses to your will or trust grants representatives the legal capacity to manage accounts.

Privacy Protection: Utilizing secure password managers avoids the public exposure of sensitive login credentials in court.

◇ PART 8 ◇

Trust Administration After Death

Guides successor trustees and families through the basic responsibilities after the trust creator dies.

CHAPTER 42

First Steps for the Successor Trustee

SELECTING KEY DECISION-MAKERS forms the foundational step in establishing a functional and resilient estate plan. The alignment of these core roles determines the efficiency of daily asset management and the integrity of future property transitions. Grantors must carefully evaluate the personal qualifications, availability, and willingness of those they nominate to serve as trustees. Appointing individuals who possess a strong sense of responsibility and financial administrative skills supports the stable execution of your long-term intentions. This protective planning provides your family with a clear path forward, securing your assets and ensuring your instructions are followed with complete fidelity. The everyday coordination of your assets remains entirely within your personal preview, providing uninterrupted access to your holdings. This reliable operational layout ensures that the transition to a trust structure supports your ongoing lifestyle and long-term security goals.

> First steps in successor administration involve securing physical property, locating original estate planning documents, obtaining certified copies of the death certificate, and notifying essential financial and governmental institutions.

DOCUMENT SPOTLIGHT: THE TRUSTEE AFFIDAVIT

Purpose: To formally declare that you have accepted the role of successor trustee and possess the active authority to manage the trust's portfolio.

Key Authority: This recorded document allows you to retitle financial accounts, manage real property, and conduct daily business transactions on behalf of the trust.

Securing the Estate and Finding Documents

Securing the grantor's real estate and personal property represents your first physical responsibility as a successor trustee. This task involves changing door locks, checking security systems, and securing personal belongings held within the family home. The trustee must compile an inventory of all tangible items to protect the estate from loss or unauthorized distribution. Having these physical spaces secured provides a stable foundation for the administrative tasks that follow.

Locating the original estate planning documents is the next critical step in establishing your active authority over the trust assets. You must search the grantor's personal files, safe deposit boxes, or coordinate with their legal advisors to find the original trust agreement and any pour-over wills. Presenting these original documents allows the successor trustee to verify their administrative powers with financial institutions. This careful organization provides your family with a clear and unified path for settling your estate.

Common Mistake: Delaying the appointment of a successor trustee under the assumption that a single adult does not require structured support during their lifetime.

Ordering Certificates and Giving Notices

The successor trustee must secure multiple certified copies of the grantor's death certificate from the local vital statistics office or funeral director. These certified copies are required by financial institutions, land registries, insurance providers, and government agencies to verify the grantor's passing and update ownership records. Along with ordering certificates, the trustee has a legal responsibility to notify important parties, including credit reporting bureaus, social security offices, and state health departments. These timely notifications protect the estate from identity theft and stop automatic benefit payments to prevent future overpayment liabilities.

STATE LAW REMINDER

"State statutes outline specific notice requirements that successor trustees must send to all qualified beneficiaries and heirs within a designated timeframe after assuming office."

Fulfilling these notice requirements ensures complete transparency and protects the successor trustee from potential administrative disputes. Working with an experienced professional helps you maintain full compliance with all local estate notification guidelines.

KEY TAKEAWAY

Property Protection: Securing real estate and personal property prevents loss and establishes an orderly transition period.

Official Verification: Certified death certificates are required to verify the grantor's passing and update bank records.

Fiduciary Notices: Successor trustees must send formal legal notices to qualified beneficiaries according to state timelines.

CHAPTER 43

Paying Debts, Expenses, and Taxes

MANAGING THE FINANCIAL OBLIGATIONS of the trust is an essential part of settling the grantor's estate with complete legal compliance. This administrative process involves identifying outstanding liabilities, reviewing recurring monthly bills, and coordinating payments for final medical and funeral expenses. The successor trustee has a legal responsibility to satisfy valid creditor claims from the trust assets in an orderly manner. Each financial transaction must be documented systematically to protect the estate from future claims or administrative disputes. Utilizing a dedicated trust ledger establishes a reliable foundation, allowing you to track all income and expenditures with complete transparency. This careful organization provides your family with a clear path forward, securing your assets and ensuring your instructions are followed with complete fidelity. The everyday coordination of your assets remains entirely within your personal preview, providing uninterrupted access to your holdings. This reliable operational layout ensures that the transition to a trust structure supports your ongoing lifestyle and long-term security goals.

> Paying debts, expenses, and taxes is the administrative duty of the successor trustee to identify liabilities, satisfy valid claims, maintain meticulous financial records, and file final tax returns.

DOCUMENT SPOTLIGHT: THE TRUST LEDGER

Purpose: To serve as the primary accounting record for tracking all cash receipts, investment income, expenditures, and distributions.

Key Authority: This ledger provides beneficiaries and courts with clear evidence of the trustee's financial transparency and fiduciary compliance.

Managing Bills and Final Expenses

The successor trustee is responsible for identifying and paying the grantor's outstanding liabilities, including utility bills, credit card balances, and medical expenses. This task begins with reviewing the grantor's mail and digital accounts to locate recurring invoices and outstanding account statements. The trustee opens an administrative bank account using the trust's new federal tax identification number to manage cash transactions. Using this separate account keeps the trust finances fully organized and simplifies the accounting process.

Reviewing each invoice carefully ensures that you only pay valid debts from the trust's liquid resources. The trustee must pay funeral costs, final medical expenses, and ongoing property preservation costs before distributing any assets. Maintaining detailed records of these payments protects the successor trustee from personal liability and disputes. This careful documentation provides clear evidence that you are managing the estate's liabilities in an orderly manner.

Common Mistake: Paying outstanding bills immediately with personal funds or distributing assets to heirs before resolving the grantor's valid creditor claims.

Tax Records and Fiduciary Accounting

The successor trustee must coordinate with a qualified accountant to file the grantor's final personal income tax returns and any fiduciary income tax returns for the trust. This process requires gathering complete records of the grantor's income, capital gains, and deductible expenses for the year of their passing. The trustee also tracks the trust's internal earnings and expenses during the administration period to report them accurately. Filing these tax returns on time protects the trust assets from interest charges and federal penalties, securing the value of the estate for your beneficiaries.

STATE LAW REMINDER

"State regulations define the priority order for paying estate claims and outline the specific deadlines for filing state inheritance or estate tax returns."

Working closely with an experienced professional ensures that your tax filings are completed in complete accordance with local guidelines. This proactive compliance shields the successor trustee from potential audits and preserves the financial integrity of the estate.

KEY TAKEAWAY

Administrative Accounts: Opening separate trust checking accounts keeps all cash receipts and payments fully organized.

Priority Payments: Successor trustees must satisfy funeral costs, administrative expenses, and valid taxes prior to distribution.

Meticulous Tracking: Maintaining systematic accounting ledgers protects fiduciaries from personal liability and beneficiary disputes.

CHAPTER 44

Distributing Trust Property

COMPLETING THE ASSET DISTRIBUTION PROCESS represents the final administrative milestone in executing the grantor's estate plan. This final transition involves transferring the legal title of real estate, financial accounts, and personal belongings directly to the designated heirs. The successor trustee must follow the specific instructions outlined in the trust agreement exactly as written. Appointing a responsible representative to coordinate these transfers ensures that the estate is settled privately and in an orderly manner. Utilizing a structured receipt and release framework protects the trustee from future liabilities while maintaining complete transparency. This methodical alignment supports family harmony during a sensitive transition, ensuring your legacy is preserved with complete legal clarity. The everyday coordination of your assets remains entirely within your personal preview, providing uninterrupted access to your holdings. This reliable operational layout ensures that the transition to a trust structure supports your ongoing lifestyle and long-term security goals.

> Distributing trust property is the private, legal process of transferring the remaining funded assets from the trust to the designated beneficiaries according to the trust agreement.

DOCUMENT SPOTLIGHT: RECEIPT AND RELEASE

Purpose: To formally document a beneficiary's acceptance of their distribution and release the trustee from further liability.

Key Authority: This executed document confirms that the beneficiary is satisfied with the trust accounting and completes their active participation.

Transferring Assets to Beneficiaries

The successor trustee coordinates the transfer of different asset classes, including executing new deeds for real estate and retitling financial accounts. The trustee reviews the trust agreement to determine whether distributions are outright transfers or structured ongoing payments. Outright transfers require preparing legal documents, such as quitclaim deeds or account transfer forms, to convey ownership directly to the heirs. This process must be conducted in a highly systematic manner to protect the value of the estate.

Preparing these legal transfers carefully ensures that your distributions comply fully with the terms of the trust agreement. The trustee must obtain signed receipts and liability releases from each beneficiary before distributing the respective assets. Securing these executed release forms protects the successor trustee from potential retroactive claims and disputes. This methodical coordination ensures that all parties are satisfied with the final settlement of the trust portfolio.

! **Common Mistake:** Transferring valuable trust assets to beneficiaries before securing signed receipt and release forms, which can leave the trustee exposed to future claims.

Fostering Harmony and Reducing Conflict

Maintaining complete transparency and open communication represents an effective strategy for successor trustees to promote family harmony. The trustee provides all qualified beneficiaries with regular administrative updates, financial accountings, and clear timelines for distributions. Sharing these administrative details reduces the potential for misunderstandings and helps family members feel completely supported. This collaborative approach protects the family legacy from conflict and ensures a peaceful transition of wealth.

STATE LAW REMINDER

"State statutes govern the specific duties of a successor trustee, including mandatory accounting requirements and notice provisions that must be sent to all qualified beneficiaries during trust administration."

Aligning your trust funding with local marital property regulations ensures that your estate plans remain fully compliant and secure. Consulting with experienced estate professionals helps you structure your trust to prevent potential disputes among family members. This careful alignment provides a clear and harmonious path forward that respects the rights of each family member.

KEY TAKEAWAY

Outright Transfers: Preparing new deeds and retitling account registrations coordinates the transfer of trust property directly to heirs.

Friction Reduction: Outlining precise administrative rules prevents family misunderstandings during the settlement process.

Independent Management: Utilizing professional trustees ensures objective and fair execution of trust instructions.

PART 9

Taxes, Protection, and Advanced Planning

Explains tax basics, common misunderstandings, creditor issues, and situations that may require advanced legal advice.

CHAPTER 45

Estate Taxes in 2026

UNDERSTANDING THE FEDERAL TRANSFER TAX SYSTEM is an essential part of organizing a comprehensive estate plan for high-net-worth families. The federal government imposes an estate tax on the transfer of a deceased person's taxable estate, which is calculated based on the gross value of all property owned or controlled at the time of death. The threshold for this tax is subject to statutory adjustments, and keeping track of these annual adjustments represents an important task for individuals with significant holdings. This structured planning allows families to evaluate their potential tax exposure and implement legal strategies to minimize future liabilities. By organizing your assets under a unified plan, you provide clear guidance for your successor trustee and secure your family's financial legacy. This systematic approach ensures that your estate remains fully compliant with current tax laws while preparing a private and efficient transfer for your heirs. The everyday coordination of your assets remains entirely within your personal preview, providing uninterrupted access to your holdings. This reliable operational layout ensures that the transition to a trust structure supports your ongoing lifestyle and long-term security goals.

> The federal estate tax is a transfer tax levied on the taxable value of an estate at death that exceeds the statutory exemption threshold, requiring precise valuation and professional coordination for high-net-worth families.

DOCUMENT SPOTLIGHT: THE ESTATE TAX RETURN

Purpose: To report the total value of the gross estate, document deductions, and calculate any federal transfer tax liability.

Key Authority: This formal IRS filing, known as Form 706, must be completed and submitted by the executor or trustee within nine months of the grantor's passing.

Federal Estate Tax Exemptions and Exclusions

The federal estate tax operates with a lifetime exemption amount that determines whether an estate is subject to the transfer tax. Assets valued below this statutory exclusion amount pass to heirs free of federal estate taxes, keeping administration straightforward for most estates. For estates exceeding this threshold, the tax rates can be significant, requiring careful asset valuation and professional coordinate planning to preserve the value of the portfolio. Working with experienced estate tax attorneys and certified public accountants ensures that your asset valuations are accurate and fully documented.

Systematically organizing your financial records during your lifetime supports an efficient tax reporting process for your successor trustee. Your representatives must secure qualified professional appraisals for real estate, business interests, and investment holdings as of the date of death to establish these values. This thorough preparation ensures that all tax filings comply fully with federal guidelines and protects the estate from unexpected audits. Maintaining this continuous organization preserves your accumulated wealth and establishes a resilient baseline for your family.

Common Mistake: Believing that federal estate tax exemptions are permanently fixed, when in fact statutory guidelines permit these thresholds to adjust or sunset based on legislative timelines.

State-Level Estate Taxes and Professional Guidance

Along with the federal tax system, several state jurisdictions impose independent estate or inheritance taxes with separate exemption thresholds that are often lower than the federal limit. An individual may own property in a state that levies these local transfer taxes, which requires specialized planning to protect the estate from unexpected local tax burdens. Coordinating your trust funding to address these state-specific codes ensures that your assets are distributed in a highly efficient manner. Seeking professional guidance from qualified tax advisors helps you navigate these overlapping regulations and secure your family legacy.

STATE LAW REMINDER

"Individual states govern their own estate and inheritance tax codes, establishing distinct exemption limits, tax rates, and filing deadlines that operate independently of the federal system."

Working with experienced professionals allows you to structure your estate plan to comply fully with both state and federal tax regulations. This active coordination protects your personal wealth and ensures that your chosen representatives feel completely prepared to manage tax transitions during the settlement process.

KEY TAKEAWAY

Federal Transfer Tax: Federal estate taxes are imposed on estates exceeding the lifetime statutory exemption threshold.

State Tax Codes: Some states levy independent estate or inheritance taxes with lower exemption limits.

Professional Coordination: High-net-worth families require experienced tax professionals to compile valuations and file returns correctly.

CHAPTER 46

Does a Living Trust Reduce Taxes?

ADDRESSING THE TAX IMPLICATIONS OF TRUST OWNERSHIP is a fundamental part of developing a realistic and legally compliant estate plan. A common misunderstanding suggests that establishing a basic revocable living trust automatically reduces your personal income tax obligations or eliminates estate taxes. In reality, a revocable living trust is a tax-neutral instrument that does not alter your tax status during your lifetime. The grantor remains responsible for reporting all income and capital gains generated by trust assets on their personal tax return. Understanding this tax neutrality allows you to coordinate your financial accounts and real estate holdings with complete accuracy. This structured planning ensures that your estate remains fully compliant with state and federal guidelines while providing private, court-free asset transitions. The everyday coordination of your assets remains entirely within your personal preview, providing uninterrupted access to your holdings. This reliable operational layout ensures that the transition to a trust structure supports your ongoing lifestyle and long-term security goals.

> A basic revocable living trust is a tax-neutral entity during the grantor's lifetime, maintaining the grantor's personal social security number for all tax reporting and financial transactions.

DOCUMENT SPOTLIGHT: TAX IDENTIFICATION FORM

Purpose: To verify that the revocable living trust utilizes the grantor's personal social security number for tax reporting.

Key Authority: This form, typically a W-9, is submitted to financial institutions to establish the tax-neutral status of the trust accounts.

The Principle of Lifetime Tax Neutrality

Because the grantor retains complete control to amend, fund, or revoke the trust at any time, the Internal Revenue Service treats the trust as a transparent entity for income tax purposes. All income, dividends, and capital gains earned by funded accounts are reported directly under the grantor's social security number, keeping your annual tax filing identical to individual reporting. This seamless integration ensures that establishing a trust does not add complex tax reporting requirements or require a separate tax identification number during your lifetime. You continue to file standard individual income tax returns, maintaining your existing deductions, exemptions, and filing schedules with standard administrative ease.

Coordinating your financial accounts with this tax-neutral structure keeps your ongoing administrative tasks simple and straightforward. You do not need to file a separate fiduciary tax return for the trust while you are alive and mentally capable of managing your affairs. This integrated structure ensures that your assets remain fully accessible to you, supporting your daily lifestyle and investment activities. Properly aligning these accounts provides peace of mind, knowing that your financial routine proceeds without disruption.

Common Mistake: Believing that transferring personal assets into a revocable living trust allows you to claim new income tax deductions or avoid filing standard personal tax returns.

Post-Death Tax Reporting and Fiduciary Obligations

Upon the passing of the grantor, the revocable living trust becomes irrevocable, transforming into a separate legal entity for tax purposes. The successor trustee must obtain a unique employer identification number for the trust to report any income earned during the administration period. The trustee coordinates with a qualified accountant to file fiduciary income tax returns and distribute tax schedules to the beneficiaries. This post-death tax coordination is essential to ensure that the estate complies with all federal and state tax guidelines before final distributions are completed.

STATE LAW REMINDER

"Fiduciary tax regulations require successor trustees to file annual income tax returns for the trust if the entity earns income above the statutory minimum during the settlement period."

Ensuring that your trustee compiles accurate financial records throughout the administration period prevents tax delays and IRS penalties. This active compliance shields the successor trustee from personal liability and protects the value of the estate for your beneficiaries.

KEY TAKEAWAY

Tax Neutrality: Revocable living trusts are completely transparent for income tax purposes during the grantor's lifetime.

Social Security Number: Trust accounts utilize the grantor's personal social security number, keeping annual tax preparation simple.

Separate Entity: Trusts become independent taxable entities after the grantor's passing, requiring a unique employer identification number.

CHAPTER 47

Asset Protection and Revocable Trusts

EVALUATING THE LEVEL OF CREDITOR PROTECTION offered by different estate planning structures represents a critical part of securing your family assets. A common misunderstanding suggests that transferring property into a basic revocable living trust shields those assets from personal lawsuit claims and creditor collection activities. In reality, because the grantor maintains complete control and continuous access to the trust assets, the law treats the grantor as the personal owner of the property. This ongoing control keeps the trust assets exposed to any valid legal claims or judgments against the creator. Understanding these functional boundaries is essential to design an effective estate plan that provides realistic protections for your family. Utilizing a revocable trust is a highly effective way to bypass probate court privately, but achieving robust creditor insulation requires exploring alternative legal structures. The everyday coordination of your assets remains entirely within your personal preview, providing uninterrupted access to your holdings. This reliable operational layout ensures that the transition to a trust structure supports your ongoing lifestyle and long-term security goals.

> A revocable living trust does not provide asset protection from personal creditors during the grantor's lifetime, as the grantor's complete control keeps the assets legally accessible to satisfy outstanding judgments.

DOCUMENT SPOTLIGHT: TRUST SCHEDULE OF ASSETS

Purpose: To list and identify all personal property, financial accounts, and real estate owned by the revocable living trust.

Key Authority: This internal schedule serves to document trust funding, though it does not insulate the listed property from personal liabilities.

The Relationship Between Control and Creditor Exposure

The legal principle governing asset protection states that the level of creditor exposure is directly proportional to the amount of control the grantor retains over the property. Because a revocable trust allows you to spend, withdraw, or terminate the trust at any time, courts view the trust assets as fully accessible to you. Consequently, if a creditor obtains a legal judgment against the grantor, a judge can order the grantor to withdraw trust assets to satisfy that personal liability. This direct relationship between control and exposure means that revocable structures cannot act as a shield against personal lawsuit claims during your lifetime.

Organizing your personal and business affairs to address these creditor risks requires a thorough evaluation of your professional activities and assets. Many grantors integrate standard insurance policies, such as umbrella liability coverage, to provide a layer of protection against personal claims. Coordinating these insurance policies with your living trust ensures that your family home and savings remain secure without restricting your personal control. Maintaining this continuous protection provides peace of mind, knowing that your estate plan is supported by realistic safeguards.

Common Mistake: Assuming that transferring your primary residence or financial accounts into a revocable trust prevents creditors from filing liens against those assets during your lifetime.

Alternative Structures for Robust Asset Protection

Achieving strong insulation from creditor claims requires utilizing specialized irrevocable trust structures that permanently separate the grantor from ownership and control of the assets. Once assets are transferred into an irrevocable trust, the grantor cannot amend the agreement, retrieve the property, or serve as the active trustee. This complete separation removes the assets from the grantor's personal estate, preventing creditors from accessing them to satisfy individual judgments. Working with an experienced professional helps you determine when these advanced protective structures are appropriate for your family's needs.

STATE LAW REMINDER

"State statutes define the specific legal boundaries for asset protection, establishing distinct rules for homestead exemptions, tenancy by the entirety, and irrevocable structures."

Aligning your estate planning with these local statutes ensures that your personal property and family home are protected to the maximum extent permitted by law. This proactive coordination protects your assets and provides your family with a secure, legally compliant path forward.

KEY TAKEAWAY

Ongoing Exposure: Revocable trust assets remain accessible to the grantor's creditors due to the grantor's continuous control.

Direct Relationship: The law links asset protection to a loss of personal control, meaning only irrevocable structures provide strong insulation.

Complementary Protection: Utilizing personal liability insurance alongside a living trust provides practical protection for everyday planning.

CHAPTER 48

When You May Need an Irrevocable Trust

ESTABLISHING AN IRREVOCABLE TRUST represents a specialized planning choice designed to secure assets under a permanent legal structure. This process involves relinquishing personal ownership of specific properties to achieve distinct tax benefits or long-term protective goals. Many families utilize these entities to protect their holdings from future liability or to coordinate care options. By defining the administrative parameters in a permanent instrument, you provide direct guidance for those who will handle your affairs in future years. Each designated trustee receives a specific mandate to protect the integrity of the family estate according to the terms you outline. As a result of this meticulous planning, the structural alignment of the irrevocable trust supports a secure transition that benefits everyone involved. The everyday coordination of your assets remains entirely within your personal preview, providing uninterrupted access to your holdings. This reliable operational layout ensures that the transition to a trust structure supports your ongoing lifestyle and long-term security goals.

An irrevocable trust is a permanent legal entity established to remove assets from the grantor's personal ownership, providing robust protections for tax, medical, and legacy coordination.

DOCUMENT SPOTLIGHT: THE GIFT TRUST

Purpose: To permanently convey assets to named beneficiaries under independent fiduciary management.

Key Authority: This contract form removes the listed assets from the grantor's taxable estate, ensuring total protection from personal creditor claims.

Advanced Tax Planning and Asset Protection

Advanced tax planning often utilizes irrevocable trust structures to reduce the overall value of a taxable estate. When assets are transferred permanently into the trust, they are removed from the grantor's personal estate, reducing overall estate tax exposure. This arrangement is highly useful for high-net-worth families who want to protect their legacy from substantial transfer tax liabilities. The independent trustee manages these funds to make investment decisions and distributions in accordance with the agreement.

Establishing these advanced structures early in life provides a secure foundation for your personal security. Taking the time to discuss your goals with your designated representative prepares them to assist you effectively. Working closely with experienced estate tax professionals ensures that your asset valuations are accurate and fully documented. This meticulous planning secures your family legacy and supports your long-term wealth transfer strategies.

Common Mistake: Assuming that a revocable living trust provides the same level of tax planning and creditor protection as a specialized irrevocable trust.

LONG-TERM CARE AND CHARITABLE GIVING

Long-term care coordination represents another common reason families establish irrevocable trusts to secure support during aging. The assets transferred into a specialized protection trust are removed from personal ownership to assist with medical assistance eligibility criteria. This structured legal transfer allows individuals to qualify for essential medical support and preserve their home for family members. Coordinating these trusts with charitable giving plans also allows families to support philanthropic goals and secure immediate tax advantages.

STATE LAW REMINDER

"Local statutes govern the specific Medicaid look-back periods and asset transfer rules, requiring strict compliance to ensure benefits are preserved."

Ensuring that your trust complies with the look-back rules is essential to prevent eligibility delays for long-term care benefits. Working with an experienced elder law professional guarantees that your asset transfers are fully compliant with local guidelines. This coordinate planning protects your family from unexpected medical costs and secures your personal welfare during health transitions. Proper administration of these irrevocable funds ensures a reliable and supportive path for your heirs.

KEY TAKEAWAY

Permanent Separation: Irrevocable trusts transfer property permanently, removing the assets from the grantor's taxable estate.

Advanced Benefits: These structures provide robust protection from personal lawsuits and qualify grantors for medical assistance programs.

Professional Coordination: Designing irrevocable structures requires experienced legal guidance to ensure compliance with tax and elder law codes.

CHAPTER 49

Special Needs Planning

DESIGNING A COMPREHENSIVE ESTATE PLAN for a family member with special needs requires a highly structured and protective legal framework. This process involves the creation of a specialized trust that manages inheritance funds without affecting the beneficiary's eligibility for government assistance programs. Each designated instruction receives a specific mandate to support the preservation of your personal dignity and care. By defining these parameters in a clear instrument, you provide direct guidance for those who will oversee your physical welfare. Each step of this process is designed to protect the assets from loss or mismanagement during the settlement period. As a result of this meticulous planning, the structural alignment of the special needs trust supports a seamless transition that benefits everyone involved. The everyday coordination of your assets remains entirely within your personal preview, providing uninterrupted access to your holdings. This reliable operational layout ensures that the transition to a trust structure supports your ongoing lifestyle and long-term security goals.

> A special needs trust is a specialized fiduciary structure designed to hold assets for a disabled individual, preserving their eligibility for public assistance while funding supplemental care.

DOCUMENT SPOTLIGHT: SPECIAL NEEDS

Purpose: To establish an ongoing trust that holds inheritance assets specifically to fund supplemental personal and medical care.

Key Authority: This trust agreement authorizes the trustee to cover supplemental expenses directly without jeopardizing government assistance benefits.

Protecting Benefit Eligibility and Fiduciary Oversight

A special needs trust holds assets for the sole benefit of a disabled individual under the continuous supervision of a designated trustee. The trustee manages the funds, making distributions for supplemental needs, such as personal care, therapy, and specialized equipment. This separate ownership allows the beneficiary to receive essential inheritance support and maintain eligibility for government programs. Appointing a responsible representative to manage these funds ensures that distributions are made objectively and in accordance with your instructions.

Failing to structure these distributions correctly can lead to the immediate loss of valuable public benefits for your loved ones. Working with a qualified professional helps you identify the correct trust provisions to protect your family's financial security. The trustee coordinates all distributions to ensure compliance with strict public benefit guidelines, protecting the participant's essential supportive network. This proactive coordination provides immediate comfort, allowing your family to focus on building a secure future.

Common Mistake: Leaving a direct financial inheritance to a disabled beneficiary, which can immediately disqualify them from essential government assistance programs.

Creating a Comprehensive Care Plan

Coordinating special needs trusts with other primary estate documents creates a cohesive protective framework for your personal welfare. The trustee works in alignment with your healthcare agents to ensure that medical costs are managed responsibly. This systematic arrangement protects your personal autonomy while securing the continuous administration of your household affairs. Proper organization of these health documents ensures that your personal preferences are respected under all circumstances.

STATE LAW REMINDER

"State laws regulate the administration of special needs trusts, defining strict rules regarding what types of expenses the trustee can legally pay on behalf of the beneficiary."

Reviewing these local statutory rules ensures that your trust agreement operates successfully within your state's legal system. Regular reviews of your estate assets with a professional will help you confirm that your plan stays compliant with current regulations over time. This active management provides a secure framework that protects your family's welfare and maintains family clarity.

KEY TAKEAWAY

Government Assistance: Specialized trusts hold assets privately to protect eligibility for public support programs.

Supplemental Support: Trustees distribute funds for personal care, therapy, and technology that public benefits do not cover.

Fiduciary Responsibility: Trustees must understand complex state laws to manage distributions without disrupting benefit programs.

CHAPTER 50

Business Owners and Real Estate Investors

MANAGING BUSINESS INTERESTS and real estate investments requires a highly coordinated and resilient estate planning framework to ensure continuous operations. This process involves integrating your corporate holdings, rental properties, and limited liability companies with your personal trust structure. Having these business assets organized ensures that your personal investments and financial records remain secure during critical transitions. By defining these parameters in a clear instrument, you provide direct guidance for those who will manage these systems. Each designated representative receives a specific mandate to manage or preserve your online data according to your instructions. As a result of this meticulous planning, the structural alignment of your business succession plan supports a seamless transition that benefits everyone involved. The everyday coordination of your assets remains entirely within your personal preview, providing uninterrupted access to your holdings. This reliable operational layout ensures that the transition to a trust structure supports your ongoing lifestyle and long-term security goals.

> Business succession planning is the process of integrating corporate structures, rental real estate, and limited liability companies with your trust to secure operational continuity and protect assets.

DOCUMENT SPOTLIGHT: SUCCESSION AGREEMENT

Purpose: To formally integrate business ownership interests and operational rules with your personal living trust.

Key Authority: This binding document allows the successor trustee to assume immediate management authority over business accounts and properties.

Integrating Business Entities with Trusts

Integrating business interests with your living trust ensures that your commercial operations continue smoothly after your passing. This transition is managed privately by your successor trustee, avoiding the administrative delays and public disclosure of probate court. The successor trustee assumes immediate authority to manage company accounts, pay employees, and conduct transactions. This continuous administration protects the value of the business and maintains relationships with business partners.

Structuring buy-sell agreements with your co-owners provides a clear buyout plan if a partner passes away or becomes disabled. These written agreements establish a pre-arranged buyout structure, protecting business operations and providing financial security. Coordinating these business arrangements with your primary estate documents protects your commercial legacy and supports your partners. This thorough planning protects your accumulated wealth and supports your loved ones with complete clarity.

Common Mistake: Leaving business operating agreements and membership certificates uncoordinated with your personal living trust, forcing business assets into probate.

Management Continuity and Rental Properties

Managing rental properties within a limited liability company owned by your trust represents a highly effective asset protection strategy. The limited liability company protects your personal assets from claims arising from the rental properties. The trust serves as the owner of the company, ensuring the real estate investments bypass probate court privately. This combined layout provides a secure layer of protection for your real estate portfolio.

STATE LAW REMINDER

"State statutes regulate limited liability companies and business registries, requiring specific transfer protocols to vest ownership interests in a revocable trust."

Verifying these local corporate registration requirements ensures that your business structures are recognized as legally valid by local authorities. This active coordination protects your personal assets and supports your chosen representatives during critical administrative transitions. Properly aligning your business titles ensures that your successor trustee can manage the portfolio privately during periods of incapacity. Regular consultations with an estate professional ensure that your business and trust remain fully compliant with current state standards.

KEY TAKEAWAY

Operational Continuity: Trusts transfer business ownership privately, preventing operational pauses and financial liquidation.

Limited Liability: Holding rental real estate within an LLC owned by your trust provides dual liability protection.

Succession Plans: Integrating buy-sell agreements with your trust ensures co-owners can purchase shares fairly and directly.

CHAPTER 51

Moving to Another State After Creating a Trust

RELOCATING TO ANOTHER STATE after creating an estate plan represents a significant transition that requires a thorough review of your primary documents. Different states have distinct legal statutes governing wills, trusts, medical directives, and powers of attorney. This process involves evaluating how your existing trust agreement and complementary documents comply with local rules in your new home. Having these legal documents updated ensures that your personal values and property distributions remain fully secure under local codes. By defining these parameters in a clear instrument, you provide direct guidance for those who will handle your affairs. Each designated individual receives a specific mandate to protect the integrity of the family estate according to the terms you outline. As a result of this meticulous planning, the structural alignment of the trust supports a seamless transition that benefits everyone involved. The everyday coordination of your assets remains entirely within your personal preview, providing uninterrupted access to your holdings. This reliable operational layout ensures that the transition to a trust structure supports your ongoing lifestyle and long-term security goals.

> Trust portability is the process of reviewing and amending your estate plan after moving to ensure full compliance with the tax laws and statutory codes of your new state.

DOCUMENT SPOTLIGHT: TRUST AMENDMENT

Purpose: To modify specific provisions of your trust agreement to align with the laws of your new state.

Key Authority: This formal amendment updates out-of-state property clauses and adjusts administrative terms to comply with local regulations.

The Legal Effects of Relocation

The legal effects of relocation can impact the validity and efficiency of your existing estate planning documents. While most states recognize trusts executed validly in another state, local administrative rules and court procedures can vary significantly. This variance can affect how financial institutions, land registries, and local hospitals interpret your designated representative's authority. Preparing updated documents ensures that your personal preferences are respected under all circumstances in your new home.

Updating your financial power of attorney and healthcare directives with state-specific forms ensures immediate acceptance by local networks. This careful preparation prevents administrative delays when your agent needs to act on your behalf during health emergencies. Establishing these safeguards ensures that your personal interests are managed with complete safety and continuity. Working with an experienced professional in your new state guarantees that your files are fully organized.

!

Common Mistake: Believing that an estate plan remains fully optimized after relocation without updating powers of attorney or real estate titles in your new state.

Out-of-State Property and Document Review

Relocating also requires reviewing the titles and deeds of any real estate owned by your trust. If you sell your previous home and purchase property in your new state, you must ensure the new deed is titled directly in the name of your trust. This funding process is essential to maintain your probate avoidance goals and protect your family assets. Proper organization of these property transfers ensures that your estate remains fully secure under current local tax codes.

STATE LAW REMINDER

"State laws govern property taxes, homestead exemptions, and signature witness requirements, which directly influence trust and deed execution standards."

Ensuring your real estate deeds are recorded with local county offices is essential to legally transfer ownership to a trust. This active coordination protects your personal data and supports your chosen representatives during critical administrative transitions. Properly aligning your newly purchased properties ensures your estate plan continues to operate with complete reliability. Regular updates to your documents keep your designations aligned with current family needs and local regulations.

KEY TAKEAWAY

Statutory Variance: State-specific execution laws dictate the legal validity of powers of attorney and health directives.

Funding Portability: Real estate purchased in a new state must be formally retitled to maintain your trust's protective benefits.

Plan Optimization: Reviewing your entire estate plan after moving keeps your documents compliant with local tax and property laws.

PART 10

Your Living Trust Action Plan

Provides practical checklists and final guidance to help readers prepare for creating or updating their estate plan.

CHAPTER 52

Your Estate Planning Inventory

COMPILING A COMPREHENSIVE INVENTORY of personal assets represents a highly practical and foundational step in preparing a complete estate plan. This systematic organization allows you to catalog your valuable holdings, outstanding liabilities, and important documents in a single accessible record. Having these details organized in a structured format simplifies the work of your legal advisors and ensures that your chosen successor trustees have a clear road map. By defining these parameters in a personal memorandum, you provide direct guidance for those who will manage your affairs during transitions. Each designated item receives a specific designation to ensure complete administrative clarity for your family members. As a result of this meticulous planning, the structural alignment of your inventory supports a seamless transition that benefits everyone involved. The everyday coordination of your assets remains entirely within your personal preview, providing uninterrupted access to your holdings. This reliable operational layout ensures that the transition to a trust structure supports your ongoing lifestyle and long-term security goals.

> An estate planning inventory is a detailed, centralized directory that catalogs an individual's financial accounts, real estate properties, personal belongings, liabilities, and vital legal documents to support orderly administration.

DOCUMENT SPOTLIGHT: THE INVENTORY WORKSHEET

Purpose: To serve as a structured document that centralizes all information regarding your assets, debts, and administrative records.

Key Authority: This compiled record helps the successor trustee identify, locate, and secure your property efficiently during transitions.

Cataloging Financial Accounts and Real Estate

Listing checking accounts, savings plans, brokerage portfolios, and retirement holdings forms the first phase of creating your estate inventory. The directory should record the specific financial institutions, account numbers, and current contact information for each holding. It is helpful to designate whether accounts feature payable-on-death or joint tenancy titles to clarify their legal ownership. This detailed tracking ensures that all liquid resources are identified and managed correctly during transitions.

Gathering physical property records, including land deeds, vehicle titles, and business membership certificates, represents another essential task. You should specify the physical location of these original ownership documents to prevent your representatives from searching through extensive archives. Recording the estimated market values of these assets allows your fiduciaries to plan for potential tax or appraisal requirements. Maintaining this systematic inventory protects your family from administrative gaps and secures your long-term legacy.

Common Mistake: Failing to update your asset inventory regularly, which can lead to newly acquired property or closed accounts being mismanaged or omitted during the settlement process.

Organizing Family Information and Vital Records

Organizing personal information, including birth certificates, marriage records, and social security credentials, completes a robust planning file. The inventory should also document the contact details of your legal counsel, financial advisors, and insurance agents. This centralized list allows your successor trustee to notify important parties and coordinate professional support quickly. Keeping these records in a secure, fireproof location provides immediate guidance when assistance is required.

STATE LAW REMINDER

"State statutes determine the legal access rules for safe deposit boxes and personal records, which can influence how quickly your fiduciaries locate vital files."

Keeping copy documents of your safe deposit box authorizations helps your representatives access these storage areas without unnecessary delay. This careful preparation guarantees that your vital files remain fully secure and accessible to your chosen helpers. Centralizing these access records simplifies the work of your fiduciaries during sensitive transition periods. This systematic completion of your estate directory provides lasting clarity and security for your family.

KEY TAKEAWAY

Financial Inventory: Listing accounts, account numbers, and financial custodians coordinates the identification of liquid assets.

Property Records: Cataloging deeds, titles, and sentimental personal belongings prevents administrative delays.

Centralized Access: Keeping records in a secure, organized location provides immediate support for your fiduciaries.

CHAPTER 53

Questions to Ask an Estate Planning Attorney

GATHERING PROFESSIONAL GUIDANCE represents a critical phase in establishing a legally compliant and resilient estate plan. Working with a qualified attorney ensures that your trust agreement and complementary documents align perfectly with local regulations. This collaborative process allows you to evaluate your specific family needs and implement legal strategies to minimize future liabilities. By preparing targeted inquiries for your legal counsel, you provide direct guidance for the development of your estate documents. Each question is designed to clarify complex administrative parameters, ensuring complete structural alignment. As a result of this meticulous preparation, the final documents support a seamless transition that benefits everyone involved. The everyday coordination of your assets remains entirely within your personal preview, providing uninterrupted access to your holdings. This reliable operational layout ensures that the transition to a trust structure supports your ongoing lifestyle and long-term security goals.

> Inquiries for legal counsel involve a structured list of questions regarding attorney fees, trust funding procedures, deed preparation, tax implications, and state-specific estate rules to ensure a robust plan.

DOCUMENT SPOTLIGHT: THE ENGAGEMENT LETTER

Purpose: To formally define the scope of legal services, outline fee structures, and establish the attorney-client relationship.

Key Authority: This signed agreement outlines the specific tasks, timelines, and financial parameters of the estate planning representation.

Clarifying Fees, Costs, and Trust Funding

Clarifying the financial terms of the legal representation represents an important initial step when working with an estate planning attorney. Inquiring about flat-rate fees for complete planning packages helps you budget for legal services without unexpected hourly billing charges. You should also ask whether the fee includes ongoing consultations, document revisions, and future updates to accommodate family changes. This clear financial understanding supports a professional and cooperative relationship with your legal counsel.

Asking specific questions about the trust funding process represents another essential inquiry to ensure your plan is fully activated. You should verify whether the attorney prepares real estate deeds or if you must coordinate with county offices independently. Inquiring about the specific assistance provided for updating bank accounts and investment titles ensures that no assets are left exposed to probate court. Maintaining this administrative clarity allows your successor trustee to manage your funded assets with complete safety.

Common Mistake: Assuming that the attorney will automatically retitle your bank accounts and real estate deeds without explicit agreement, leaving your trust empty and inactive.

Understanding State-Specific Rules and Document Updates

Discussing how state-specific codes influence your estate plan is vital to ensure complete compliance with local statutes. You should inquire about state inheritance taxes, homestead regulations, and signature requirements for medical directives. Asking how often your documents should be reviewed to reflect changes in legislation or family structure keeps your plan robust. This proactive coordination ensures that your estate remains fully protected under all circumstances.

STATE LAW REMINDER

"State statutes govern the execution and validation of trusts, wills, and medical proxies, requiring strict compliance with local signature and witness standards."

Seeking professional guidance regarding these local execution standards ensures your documents remain legally valid after relocation or changing laws. This careful planning protects your family from administrative challenges and guarantees that your estate plan operates successfully. Preparing these targeted inquiries allows you to maximize the value of your legal consultations. This active coordination establishes a secure baseline and builds a resilient framework for your assets.

KEY TAKEAWAY

Fee Structures: Clarifying flat-rate billing and scope of services prevents unexpected hourly legal expenses.

Funding Support: Verifying who prepares deeds and coordinates account retitling ensures complete trust activation.

Relocation Review: Inquiring about state-specific transfer rules ensures your documents remain valid across state lines.

CHAPTER 54

Common Living Trust Mistakes to Avoid

ACHIEVING PLANNING OBJECTIVES requires a thorough understanding of the common administrative errors that can compromise your estate plan. Many individuals execute a living trust agreement but overlook the essential steps needed to activate its protective features. This oversight can leave family properties exposed to court-supervised probate administration, causing unnecessary delays and costs. By defining these potential pitfalls in a clear guide, you provide direct guidance for the continuous maintenance of your estate. Each warning is designed to protect the integrity of the family estate, maintaining complete administrative clarity. As a result of this meticulous coordination, the structural alignment of the trust supports a seamless transition that benefits everyone involved. The everyday coordination of your assets remains entirely within your personal preview, providing uninterrupted access to your holdings. This reliable operational layout ensures that the transition to a trust structure supports your ongoing lifestyle and long-term security goals.

> Trust mistakes represent common operational and structural errors, such as empty trusts, outdated beneficiary designations, unsuitable trustee selections, and missing backup plans, that can compromise your estate plan.

DOCUMENT SPOTLIGHT: TRUST REVIEW SCHEDULE

Purpose: To establish a systematic timeline for reviewing and updating your trust agreement and asset funding records.

Key Authority: This schedule guides fiduciaries in maintaining accurate records and updating beneficiary designations to reflect family changes.

The Pitfall of the Empty Vessel

An empty or unfunded trust is a common administrative mistake that occurs when a grantor signs the agreement but neglects to transfer asset titles. Real estate, financial accounts, and investment portfolios that remain titled in your individual name are subject to court-supervised probate administration after your passing. The successor trustee cannot manage or distribute property that has not been formally retitled into the name of the trust. This separation can create administrative confusion and require court intervention to resolve asset ownership.

Reviewing your asset titles regularly ensures that newly acquired property remains fully secure under the terms of the trust agreement. You must officially update your deeds, banking records, and brokerage titles to keep the trust active and funded over time. Failing to fund your trust leaves your home and savings exposed to public probate court delays and unnecessary fees. Properly aligning these asset registrations provides your family with a private, seamless transition of wealth.

Common Mistake: Believing that executing the trust agreement completes your plan, when in fact the trust remains completely empty and inactive until you formally retitle your assets.

Outdated Designations and Unsuitable Trustees

Failing to update beneficiary designations on life insurance and retirement plans is another common error that can disrupt your estate plan. Selecting a successor trustee without evaluating their long-term availability, financial skills, and personal integrity can compromise the administration of your estate. Outlining clear backup plans in the trust agreement ensures that alternate representatives can step in privately if your primary choice cannot serve. Coordinating these fiduciary roles with your family circumstances reduces the potential for misunderstandings and protects family harmony.

STATE LAW REMINDER

"State statutes govern the legal duties of successor trustees and determine the specific timelines for updating beneficiary designations after major family events."

Regularly reviewing your fiduciary appointments with an experienced legal advisor ensures your plan remains completely aligned with current regulations. This ongoing attention allows your family to complete the transition of wealth with minimal administrative stress. Correcting these minor administrative details prevents future legal complications and preserves the long-term strength of your estate plan. This thorough oversight supports a highly efficient settlement process that respects the needs of all family members.

KEY TAKEAWAY

Trust Funding: Formally retitling assets is mandatory to prevent your property from entering public probate court.

Regular Updates: Aligning beneficiary designations and trust clauses with major family events maintains plan accuracy.

Fiduciary Selection: Selecting trustees based on practical competence and appointing capable backups ensures stable estate settlement.

CONCLUSION

Leaving Clarity, Protection, and Peace of Mind

COMPLETING A COMPREHENSIVE ESTATE PLAN represents a profound act of care and foresight for the people who matter most in your life. Throughout this journey, the focus remains on organizing your assets, defining your health-care preferences, and establishing a stable path for future asset transitions. Creating these legal protections is a practical way to reduce administrative confusion and insulate your loved ones from stressful decisions during sensitive transitions. By documenting your intentions in a thorough and coordinated manner, you establish a clear roadmap that preserves your hard-earned assets. Each personal directive and trust provision coordinates to build a resilient shield around your estate, ensuring your legacy is respected.

Each element of your planning portfolio—from the revocable trust to the personal power of attorney—functions as an integrated system of support. Activating these documents through proper asset funding ensures that your family home, bank accounts, and investment portfolios remain secure under all circumstances. Fulfilling these responsibilities during your lifetime prevents the need for court-supervised probate administration and preserves family privacy. This continuous organization establishes a solid baseline for your successor trustees, allowing them to manage affairs efficiently. Making these choices early provides immediate comfort and security, allowing you to focus on enjoying life with your family.

Reflecting on the progress you have made throughout this planning process confirms that your personal estate is fully organized and prepared. Reviewing the essential milestones systematically allows you to verify that every primary document has been executed in complete accordance with local guidelines. The completion of these major planning tasks represents a highly responsible achievement that secures your long-term legacy. You can now proceed with complete confidence, knowing that your loved ones are protected from unexpected administrative challenges. Having these verified documents securely filed provides a reliable and supportive framework that honors your personal intentions.

Completed Estate Planning Checklist:

☒ Revocable Living Trust

☒ Last Will and Testament

☒ Financial and Durable Powers of Attorney

☒ Health Care Proxies and Directives

☒ Account Beneficiary Designation Forms

☒ Real Estate Deeds and Asset Titles

Ultimately, a complete estate plan is a valuable gift of clarity, protection, and peace of mind for future generations. Your careful coordination of assets, liabilities, and vital records ensures that your family can navigate transitions with confidence and support. This ongoing dedication to organizing your affairs preserves your accumulated wealth and establishes a peaceful environment for your heirs. By securing these essential legal safeguards today, you establish a lasting legacy of stability and responsibility. This thoughtful planning provides your loved ones with a secure and harmonious path forward for many years to come.